What Does Quebec Want?

ANDRE BERNARD

◆

What Does Quebec Want?

James Lorimer & Company, Publishers
Toronto 1978

ISBN 0-88862-139-6 Cloth
      0-88862-138-8 Paper

James Lorimer & Company, Publishers
Egerton Ryerson Memorial Building
35 Britain Street
Toronto, Ontario
Design by Don Fernley
Printed and bound in Canada

Canadian Cataloguing in Publication Data

Bernard, André, 1939-
    What does Quebec want?

Bibliography: p.
ISBN 0-88862-139-6 bd. ISBN 0-88862-138-8 pa.

1. Quebec (Province)—Politics and government—1960-   I. Title.

FC2925.2.B47   971.4'04   C77-001791-6
F1034.2.B47

Contents

List of Figures and Tables

PREFACE

A year ago I was discussing with several publishers the idea of translating and publishing a number of books devoted to Quebec elections and political parties which had appeared in 1976. In every case, the response was that what was really needed was a book which would give English-speaking readers the answer to the perennial question of the sixties and seventies: What does Quebec want? What was required was a book on Quebec written expressly for an English-speaking audience. The author would have to be someone who, born and educated in French-speaking Quebec, could identify with the dominant attitudes of the Quebecois people, and yet also be a non-partisan professional observer of Quebec politics who could take into account the varied forces at work in the province. I decided to undertake such a book.

The original manuscript was written in "bilingual" English. I am most grateful for the assistance of my editor, Robert Chodos, in rendering that draft into what I hope is a more colloquial and informal style.

André Bernard

INTRODUCTION

On November 15, 1976, a nationalist party, the Parti Québécois, gained a majority of the seats in the Quebec National Assembly. It was the fourth time in the history of Quebec that a new nationalist party dedicated to the "liberation" of French Canadians had won a parliamentary majority. It occurred first in the 1830s, with the Parti Patriote; it occurred again in the 1880s, with the Parti National; again, in the 1930s, with the Union Nationale party; and finally, on November 15, 1976, with the Parti Québécois.

Approximately 50 years elapsed between the first and second events, between the second and third, and between the third and today. Each of the first three nationalist parties, once in office, met with very strong opposition to the constitutional changes it was calling for. Each time, the English-speaking leaders of Canada were able to contain the nationalist movement and to mobilize a majority of French-speaking voters against any extreme solution.

The Parti Patriote, although successful in gaining a majority of seats, eventually met with failure. Formed in 1828 by the republicans and democrats of the period, lawyers, doctors, journalists and merchants, and led by a brilliant, well-educated and rich seigneur, Louis-Joseph Papineau, the Parti Patriote was unable to obtain parliamentary control over public expenditures and the other concessions it wanted. Emboldened by its large majority of seats in the Legislative Assembly and by the numerical superiority of French-speaking Canadians in Quebec (then known as Lower Canada), the Parti Patriote tried to achieve its objectives through rebellion. In 1836 and 1837 the party leaders organized groups of armed rebels, who started to harass British officials and soldiers who ventured outside the cities. In the fall of 1837 the British Governor of the colony sent his troops against the rebels. Parliamentary institutions and civil liberties were ignored in order to restore the security of the British settlers. The rebels were defeated, their houses destroyed, and their leaders put to death or banished from Canada while many others were thrown in jail. The Parti Patriote was disbanded and its outlawed leaders disappeared from the political scene along with their dreams of a Republic of Quebec modelled on the United States.

Finally, to crown their repression of the French nationalist movement in Canada, the Colonial Office and the British Parliament forbade the use of French in the government of the United Canadas. The defeat of the Parti Patriote had thus led to a severe setback for French Canadians and it took them many years to regain their lost language rights.

The second nationalist party to gain a majority of seats in the Quebec Assembly was the Parti National which took office in 1886, 50 years after the rebellion in Lower Canada. Like its earlier counterpart, the Parti National met with failure.

In 1886, a small minority of Parti National activists, and at least one newspaper editor, Jules-Paul Tardivel (editor of the weekly *La Vérité*), were in favor of the secession of Quebec from Canada.* These anti-federalists were convinced that there was no hope for the survival of the French-Canadian nation except in Quebec, where French Canadians at the time (as today) accounted for 80 per cent of the population. Since French Canadians were outnumbered in the institutions of the federal government, there seemed to be no hope for pro-French-Canadian federal policies. Indeed, by remaining within Canada where they were being submerged by British immigration, French Canadians faced gradual minoritization: 50 years earlier, they had been 80 per cent of the population in their "country"; the union of Lower and Upper Canada had reduced the proportion to 50 per cent, and now, in less than ten years, British immigration had succeeded in making French Canadians a minority in their own country. In 1887, French Canadians, although 80 per cent of Quebec's population, accounted for only 30 per cent of Canada's. The future for French Canadians in Canada looked very gloomy. A sample of what was awaiting them had just been given by the governments of Manitoba and New Brunswick, which had deprived French Canadians of their schools and were

---

* In *Le colonialisme au Québec* (Montreal: Editions R-B, 1966), André d'Allemagne refers to "le gouvernement nationaliste et quasi-sépara-tiste d'Honoré Mercier" ("the nationalist and quasi-separatist government of Honoré Mercier"), page 50.

imposing on them an education that was English and non-Catholic. In spite of this, the nationalist leaders of 1886 were unable to convince the voters who had supported the Parti National to go on to support their proposals for constitutional change.

The English-speaking elite, in power in the federal capital and in command of finance, trade and industry, was prompt in reacting to the threat of French-Canadian nationalism. Soon after the election of 1886, Canadian banks refused to award new loans to the nationalist government of Quebec on the grounds that the public debt of the province was six times as large as its annual revenue. Premier Honoré Mercier, leader of the Parti National, had to turn to foreign money markets for loans. The Conservative party, which Mercier had defeated, counter-attacked by trying to discredit the nationalist leaders and by pointing out to French Canadians that their nation, the French-Canadian nation, extended well beyond the boundaries of Quebec.

This was the view of the traditional elite of French Canada and particularly of the Catholic Church. In the preceding 20 years thousands of French Canadians had emigrated to other parts of North America, so that many inhabitants of Quebec had relatives or friends outside the province. In 1887, a third of all French Canadians were living outside Quebec, roughly ten per cent having settled in Ontario, ten per cent on the Prairies, and ten per cent in the United States. Most French Canadians in Quebec could not conceive of a "nation" divided, with two thirds of the French Canadians living within a sovereign Republic of Quebec and one third outside. The majority supported a strong nationalist stand in favor of French Canadians outside Quebec in matters of language and education, and had given their votes to the Parti National for this reason. However, they were not ready to follow those Parti National leaders who made speeches (for example at a celebrated meeting held on the Champ-de-Mars in the centre of Montreal) saying that if French Canadians could not have their language rights respected a Republic of Quebec should be created.

Indeed, as soon as he faced the reality of power, Mercier found that he could not count on the electorate in a stand against the federal government aimed at changing the constitutional status of Quebec. French Canadians were not ready to abandon the dream of a brilliant future in a Canada extending from coast to coast and many considered the Province of Quebec too small a territory for them.

Every year, thousands of French Canadians had to leave the province in order to find a job or a piece of land to till. Although Mercier and his nationalist colleagues felt unable to take a firm constitutional stand they made solid autonomist pleas. They asked for reforms, requested guarantees for French Canadians outside Quebec and tried to use the provincial government finances, already burdened with debts, to help develop the economy of the province. But they made no actual move toward separation.

The Liberal party, in opposition in Ottawa and led by a French Canadian, Wilfrid Laurier, adopted some of the demands of the Quebec nationalists. Laurier promised guarantees for French Canadians outside Quebec who wanted to remain French and Catholic and have their children educated in French by Catholic teachers. At the same time he made a pledge to uphold provincial rights. In so doing, he gained the favor of a majority of Quebec voters in the federal election of 1891 and recruited several of Mercier's supporters.

In the meantime, the Conservative party, in power in Ottawa, gave its Quebec provincial section the means to defeat the Parti National at the polls. Scandals involving nationalist leaders were "revealed" and investigated by the federal government.

The federal Conservatives accentuated their pressure against the Mercier government by using their control over federal institutions in the province. The Lieutenant-Governor of the province, Réal Angers, an appointee of the federal government and a former Conservative minister, refused to sign financial warrants proposed by the nationalist government, using as a pretext the scandals and the financial problems of the province. Eventually, in the provincial election of 1892, Mercier and his supporters lost power and the defeat brought about the disappearance of the Parti National.

The victory of the Liberal party led by Wilfrid Laurier in the 1896 federal election deprived the nationalist minority of electoral support among moderates and marked the end of the second explosion of nationalism in French Canada. Lack of money had prevented the Parti National from developing the Quebec economy and lack of support for a strong constitutional stand had prevented it from gaining more legislative powers for the government of Quebec.

In 1936, for a third time, a newly formed nationalist party gained a majority of seats in the Quebec Assembly. The new party, the Union Nationale, had been formed less than a year earlier through the merger of the provincial Conservative party and a splinter group of members of the Legislative Assembly who had seceded from the

Liberal party in 1934 and formed the Action Libérale Nationale. Led by Maurice Duplessis, the Union Nationale was dedicated to the objective of increased provincial autonomy and called for government control over several large corporations. Its 1936 program was socially progressive and actively nationalist. Its more nationalist leaders did not hesitate to use English-speaking Canadian capitalists as scapegoats. Nevertheless, in spite of its nationalist outlook, the Union Nationale did not challenge the continuation of federalism in Canada; it was satisfied with demanding increased provincial autonomy.

Even though it was not promoting secession, the Union Nationale encountered strong opposition from a large segment of the English-speaking elite of Canada. Banks and other financial institutions were as wary of the Union Nationale government as they had been of Mercier 50 years earlier. Leaders of the Liberal party tried to depict the nationalist leaders as fascists. The proposals for reform put forward by the new party met with objections from most parts of the French-Canadian elite.

Lacking the money and the legislative powers required to achieve the reforms he had promised, Duplessis tried to placate those interests which opposed reform but approved of nationalism. In so doing he lost the support of the most nationalist of his colleagues who were in favor of socially progressive reforms. They quit the Union Nationale and revived the Action Libérale Nationale. These progressive nationalist leaders took a very strong constitutional stand. Several Action Libérale Nationale leaders had advocated the secession of Quebec from Canada in 1934 and 1935 and they spoke again to that effect in 1938 and 1939 after their split with the Union Nationale.

The Union Nationale found itself at war with many English-speaking Quebec voters who in 1939 and 1944 gave their support to the Liberal party in Quebec elections, and at the same time it found itself at war with the most socially progressive of the French-Canadian nationalists, who gave their support to the Action Libérale Nationale. In the 1939 provincial election, the Union Nationale lost 67 of its 84 seats, retaining only 39 per cent of the vote, with seven per cent going to the Action Libérale Nationale.

The victory of the Liberals in the 1939 election was a severe setback for the nationalists, and they proved unable to recover from their defeat. The Action Libérale Nationale was disbanded. Some of its members tried to reorganize under a new guise, the Bloc Populaire, and thanks to the anger raised by conscription, they were able to gain

12 per cent of the vote in the 1944 provincial election. But that second defeat was a death blow; the nationalist leaders left the political scene.

Surprisingly, the election of 1944 returned the Union Nationale to power, although it polled only 38 per cent of the vote, one per cent less than in 1939. This phenomenon was explained by its good showing in rural areas, which were glaringly overrepresented in the Quebec Assembly. Back in power, the Union Nationale was a moderately nationalist government careful to placate rural interests and strongly opposed to federal centralization.

After the defeats of 1939 and 1944, Quebec nationalists kept silent or worked within the Union Nationale or the Liberal party. The nationalists in the Liberal party were able, in 1955, to split the party into separate federal and provincial organizations. The provincial organization became known as the Fédération Libérale du Québec and later as the Quebec Liberal party. In 1960, the Quebec Liberals, with such nationalists as René Lévesque in their ranks, were able to oust the Union Nationale from power. Nationalist members of the new Liberal government undertook some of the reforms that had been promised in 1936 by the Union Nationale. Electric power was nationalized, social security was extended, and the system of education was reorganized.

In the early 1960s, most progressive nationalists were supporters of the Liberal government in Quebec, but a minority of very young intellectuals, largely unaware of the adventure of the 1930s, felt that the problems of French Canada could not be solved without Quebec's becoming an independent state, separate from Canada. Their reasoning was similar to that of nationalists who had came to the same conclusion in the 1830s, 1880s and 1930s.

The leaders of this minority explained their viewpoints in a series of little books which had considerable influence: *Is Quebec a Colony?* and *I Chose Independence* by Raymond Barbeau, *Why I am a Separatist* by Marcel Chaput, *Colonialism in Quebec* by André d'Allemagne, *White Niggers of America* by Pierre Vallières and others. These new nationalist leaders formed numerous organizations, and although most of these did not last, two were able to present candidates in the Quebec election of 1966: the Rassemblement pour l'Indépendance Nationale and the Ralliement National. Together the nationalist candidates of these two parties got nine per cent of the popular vote, a total similar to those of the Action Libérale Nationale in 1939 and the Bloc Populaire in 1944. This time, however, the objectives were clear:

the nationalists wanted Quebec to become a sovereign state, with a flag, an anthem and a seat in the United Nations.

The two small nationalist parties had taken their votes mainly from new voters and from former Liberals. The Quebec Liberal party found itself in 1966 with 47 per cent of the vote, a loss of nine per cent from 1962. The Union Nationale, which had been defeated in 1960 with 47 per cent of the vote, now found itself in power with 41 per cent. Once again, the good showing of the Union Nationale in the overrepresented rural areas had given it a majority of seats (56 out of 108) with fewer votes than its main opponent.*

After the defeat of the Liberal party, members of the party who were strong nationalists tried to convert their colleagues to a more nationalist program. The best known of these Liberal nationalists was René Lévesque, the former minister who had led the campaign for the nationalization of the province's electric power companies in 1962. Lévesque presented a proposal that Quebec become a sovereign state within an economic association with the rest of Canada to a Liberal party convention in Quebec City in the fall of 1967. It was turned down. As a consequence, Lévesque and the few other nationalists resigned from the party.

A few weeks later, on November 18, 1967, Lévesque made public a decision he and his supporters had arrived at: they were forming a new organization called the Mouvement Souveraineté-Association (Sovereignty-Association Movement), with the objective of uniting all Quebec nationalists on the proposal that had just been discarded by the Liberal party: full sovereignty for Quebec, and economic association with the rest of Canada. Lévesque's ideas were detailed in a book entitled *Option Québec*, which appeared in bookstores in January 1968. That book was one of the bestsellers of the 1960s. It was read and sanctioned by so many members of the two older nationalist parties that pressure from within eventually led these parties to join the Mouvement Souveraineté-Association. The merger of the nationalist parties gave birth to a new organization, the Parti Québécois, founded officially on October 14, 1968.

The next provincial election, held in April 1970, revealed to Canadians outside Quebec that the separatist movement could no longer be termed a "fad"—the Parti Québécois reaped 24 per cent of the vote. From then on support for the Parti Québécois increased steadily, as

* Election statistics for the period 1935-1976 appear in table 7.

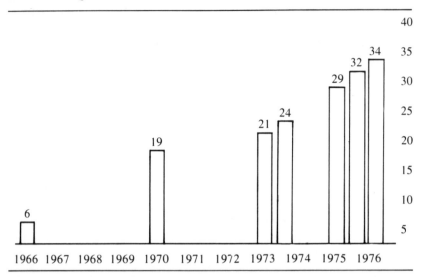

Figure 1   Growth of Support for Nationalist Parties in Quebec, According to the Elections of 1966 (6), 1970 (19), 1973 (24) and 1976 (34) and According to Pre-election Surveys Published in 1973 (21), 1975 (29) and 1976 (32). Figures are percentages based on total numbers of registered electors (not only those who cast ballots).

shown in the results of surveys and in the polling booths (see figure 1).

On November 15, 1976, for the fourth time in the history of Quebec, a newly formed nationalist party gained a majority of seats in the Quebec Assembly. Nine years after its birth, the Parti Québécois was able to muster the support of 41 per cent of Quebec voters and win 71 of the 110 seats in the Quebec National Assembly. This fourth attempt to "liberate" French Canadians may turn out to be no more successful than the previous ones. The victory of the Parti Québécois in 1976 has indeed much in common with the electoral success of the Parti Patriote in the 1830s, the Parti National in the 1880s and the Union Nationale in the 1930s. Just as in the previous cases, it is clear that a substantial number of voters gave support to the nationalist party not because they approved of its nationalist platform but because they disapproved of the other parties.

Up to 1977 surveys have shown that fewer than 20 per cent of Quebec respondents polled say they would favor complete "separation" of Quebec from the rest of Canada. The data are shown in the table.

Table 1–Opinions of the Adult Population of Quebec on the Issue of the Separation of Quebec from the Rest of Canada, 1962-1977

Year	Percentage in favor	Percentage against	Percentage undecided	Total	Number of respondents
1962	8	73	19	100	998
1965	7	79	14	100	6.910
1968	10	72	18	100	746
1969	11	75	14	100	367
1970 (spring)	14	76	10	100	820
1970 (autumn)	11	74	15	100	1.974
1972	10	68	22	100	778
1973	17	64	19	100	1.006
1974	15	74	11	100	349
1976	18	58	24	100	1.095
1977	32	52	16	100	(not available)

Source: Data collected by Maurice Pinard and Richard Hamilton from various surveys and (except for 1977 figures) published November 10, 1976 in Montreal's *Le Devoir* and *The Gazette* and the *Toronto Star*. Questions included the word "separation" except in 1977 when the question read: "The Parti Québécois wants Quebec to become an independent country associated economically with the rest of Canada. If the government of Quebec were able to establish such an economic association with the rest of Canada, would you then vote in a referendum for or against Quebec becoming an independent country?"

A survey published November 10, 1976, five days before the election, showed that, among 309 respondents who stated they favored the Parti Québécois, 158 (or 52 per cent) approved of separation, 79 (25 per cent) were opposed and 72 (23 per cent) were undecided or unclear on this subject. If the surveys can be trusted, and usually they can within a small margin of error, it is safe to say that more that one third of those who voted for a Parti Québécois candidate on November 15, 1976 were *at best* undecided on the question of independence, fewer than two thirds of Parti Québécois voters being in favor of Quebec's "separating" from Canada.

However, in spite of the similarities between the events of today and those of earlier generations, contemporary circumstances differ from those of the 1830s, 1880s or 1930s. One cannot conclude from past events that the present attempt at Quebec separation will necessarily succeed. But it is possible to analyse the causes of the contemporary unrest in Quebec, and to study the various solutions considered by those who hope to solve the problems that lie at the roots of Quebec discontent.

The objective of this short book is just that: to analyse the causes of Quebec discontent and study the various proposed solutions, including independence, that parties have put forward. The data presented here should enable one to understand better what Quebec does want, and to figure out whether extreme solutions such as the separation of Quebec from Canada will prevail over compromise and conciliation.

PART I: WHAT?

Introduction

The six largest political parties competing in the 1976 election considered Quebec to be in a crisis from at least three viewpoints: cultural, economic, and social. Although leaders of these parties disagreed on many things, they all underlined the same problems and seemed to pursue the same long-term objectives. There were, in particular, two major objectives on which all the parties agreed:

• They were pledged to ensure the survival of French in Quebec.
• They said that they favored economic prosperity for Quebec and increased control of the Quebec economy by Quebecers.

When asked the question, "What does Quebec want?" all party leaders give similar answers on the issue of basic objectives. This statement of objectives is not the whole answer, but it is the core of it.

1

National Survival

No political leader in Quebec would dare voice a doubt about the sacrosanct objective of "la survivance française en Amérique". Survival of the French-Canadian people is an obligation, an article of faith. It has been so for 200 years. It is basic, fundamental. Yet, outside Quebec, many people find it hard to understand how it can be a worthwhile objective to pursue. Unaware of the existence, in Quebec, of a French "nation" (in the sociological sense of the word), outsiders often have the same attitude toward French Canadians as they do toward their own local minorities. And the prevailing view concerning ethnic or linguistic minorities is that they should "assimilate" into the majority.

The Economics and Politics of Unilingualism

The decision to "assimilate" minorities is based on sound economic calculation. Indeed the cost of maintaining minority language rights in a country leads most states to impose one common language within their frontiers. The main argument in favor of unilingualism follows from the fact that language barriers are costly to maintain, and that their maintenance is an impediment to trade and the production of goods and services. To maintain two or more languages in one country implies costs in education: the money, energy and time devoted to second-language teaching could be used for technical training and thus could produce benefits in terms of goods and services available, or else could be saved altogether. To maintain two or more languages in one country also implies costs in communications: the direct costs of translation and of duplicate or triplicate versions of any message, and the indirect costs of delays, repetitions and misunderstandings. Language barriers, moreover, hinder social and territorial mobility and, consequently, tend to maintain inequalities, while reducing adaptability to change.

Although the benefits of unilingualism are obvious, it is not always possible to impose assimilation on a minority because the short-run costs to the minority of assimilation can be much higher than the costs of language barriers. In other words, forced assimilation is not always desirable from an economic or political viewpoint. Although the existence of minorities identified by a distinct language fosters division and conflict in a country, it may sometimes seem advisable to protect minority language rights, especially if the minority concerned is large and concentrated territorially.

Such a linguistic minority often obtains a special status within a country, its representatives being offered a certain degree of autonomy either through federalism or through legislative devolution. Such a special status enables the majority in the country to function as a unilingual "nation" while the linguistic minority, within its special status area, finds a compromise between the cost of being a separate sovereign state and the cost of undergoing assimilation, a compromise between the cultural benefits of political independence and the economic benefits of union with a larger partner.

In seeking to solve the problem created by the unwillingness of French Canadians to abandon their language, the Confederation of the British North American colonies in 1867 can be seen as such a compromise. French Canadians were given one of the Canadian provinces, Quebec. It was understood that they would control the provincial government of Quebec and legislate according to their own values in all matters relating to civil rights and education as well as local or private questions. But, in order to offer safeguards to the English-speaking minority of Quebec, the provincial government was to protect the English Protestant schools, maintain the parliamentary representation of the English-speaking areas of the province, and allow free use of the English language in the Quebec legislature and courts (articles 80, 93 and 133 of the British North America Act, 1867).

Outside Quebec, as the arrangement was understood in the 1860s, English was to remain the one and only language of the country. This was consistent with the ideology of leading English-speaking Canadians, who were trying to build a new nation in North America, a unilingual English-speaking Canadian people.

The Idea of an English-Speaking Canadian People

In the Canada defined by the leading English-speaking nationalists of the nineteenth and early twentieth centuries, there was little place for a minority language. Wherever they were a majority, English-speaking Canadians made English practically compulsory. Nowadays the arguments in favor of English run as follows: English is said to be easy to learn, clear, precise, adaptable. Its grammar is said to be much simpler than those of such languages as German, French, Spanish, Italian and Portuguese. The English language is said to convey values that promote action and productivity, while the languages spoken around the Mediterranean (French, Italian, Greek, etc.) are said to convey contemplative values, which do not meet the requirements of a modern industrialized society. English is said to be the dominant and most widely spoken language in the world; it is the official language of the richest nations (the United States, Canada, the United Kingdom, New Zealand, Australia, South Africa). In countries where English is not yet the official language, it is nevertheless a "second language" and it is taught in many schools in South America, Africa, Europe and Asia.

Even people who do not argue for the inherent superiority of English will hold that simple realism makes it necessary for French Canadians to become English-speaking. English is the language of North America and the expansion of trade and industrial capitalism favors the growth of English. The largest corporations of the world and most multinational corporations of all sizes are owned or managed by English-speaking people. In order to get the best-paid jobs, the ones offered by the large corporations, one has to speak English. A great many English-speaking Canadians seem to know only one thing in matters of language: no language is worth spending time and money on, but English. And for them it is an appalling experience to learn that millions of dollars of Canadian taxpayers' money are spent to promote French in Canada.

Up to the 1940s, wherever they were a majority, English-speaking Canadians deprived the French-speaking minorities of public school facilities in their language and forbade the use of French in governmental institutions (see box). In the British North America Act (1867), there was no mention of French except for Article 133:

> Either the English or the French Language may be used by any Person in the Debates of the Houses of the Parliament of Canada

French Language and School Rights Outside Quebec (1860–1930)

1864—Nova Scotia: French-speaking Catholic Acadians are forbidden to have French schools.

1871—New Brunswick: Catholic schools are closed and the teaching of French (and in French) is forbidden in public schools.

1877—Prince Edward Island: Catholic and French schools become outlawed.

1890—Manitoba: Separate (Catholic) schools are outlawed and the teaching of French (and in French) is forbidden at the secondary level.

1892—Northwest Territories (including what is now Alberta and Saskatchewan): Teaching in French is outlawed in public schools and Catholic schools are prohibited.

1905—Alberta and Saskatchewan: The regulations of 1892 (Northwest Territories) are confirmed.

1912—Keewatin: Denominational (Catholic) schools are suppressed and the teaching of French is forbidden.

1915—Ontario: By regulation (regulation No. 17), French is outlawed in Ontario schools.

1916—Manitoba: The teaching of French is forbidden at all levels.

1930—Saskatchewan: The teaching of French is prohibited even outside school hours.

Source: Abbé Lionel Groulx, *L'Enseignement français au Canada* (Montreal: Granger Frères, 1935).

Note: After World War I, most provincial laws were amended to permit the teaching of French as a foreign language, usually for a maximum of one hour a day. Since 1960 further amendments have been introduced. French has been allowed as the language of instruction in classrooms where students are all French-speaking, but minimum requirements have been set for the teaching of English to such classrooms.

and of the Houses of the Legislature of Quebec, and both those Languages shall be used in the respective Records and Journals of those Houses; and either of those Languages may be used by any Person or in any Pleading or Process in or issuing from any Court of Canada established under this Act, and in or from all or any of the Courts of Quebec.

The Acts of the Parliament of Canada and of the Legislature of Quebec shall be printed and published in both those Languages.

From the 1920s to the 1960s, the federal government was largely unilingual, French being used solely for formal purposes in Parliament and in some governmental transactions with the French-speaking population of Quebec.*

The most drastic solution to the problem of French in Canada would be the assimilation by force or by persuasion of French Canadians, including those of Quebec, into the English-speaking majority of Canada. This solution is not even contemplated seriously by most French-speaking Canadians because it does not fit their ideology of survival as a distinct "nation", either within or outside Canada. This would be extremely costly for both present and future generations of French Canadians. In trying to apply a program of assimilation in Quebec, a government would face strong—probably violent—resistance. Assimilation of 5,500,000 French-speaking Canadians is not a realistic solution to the language problem of Canada. The idea of an English-speaking unilingual Canadian people is neither a reflection of the reality of Canada nor a possible future.

The Fight Against English Unilingualism

Leading French-speaking Canadians have always fought the idea of "assimilation" and they are doing so with renewed vigor now that French Canada has emerged as a fully developed, industrialized, modern society. During the past century, the struggle of French Canadians against English unilingualism at the provincial level culminated in a

---

* In 1944-1945, the overall proportion of French Canadians in the federal bureaucracy was 12.25 per cent. In the most senior positions, those of Deputy Minister rank, there was not a single French Canadian. Figures taken from V. Seymour Wilson and Willard A. Mullins, *Representative Bureaucracy: Linguistic Ethnic Aspects in Canadian Public Policy*, a paper prepared for the Conference on Political Change in Canada at the University of Saskatchewan, Saskatoon, March 17, 1977, 12-13.

series of crises which from time to time poisoned relationships between the two language groups. These crises were stirred up by the school policies of the English-speaking provinces, which deprived French Canadians of their Catholic and French schools. These fights on the school question were waged in one province after another by the French-speaking minorities. Each fight roused a great deal of anger, but French Canadians were the minority and up to the 1940s they lost every time.

There has also been a long and sustained resistance to the informal suppression of the French language in Canadian federal institutions: the civil service, crown corporations and the armed forces. Three times, language grievances combined with other questions to cause a serious crisis. The first of these occurred during World War I when Canadian army officers started their recruitment operations in Quebec; resentment focussed on the fact that the recruiting officers were English-speaking. The crisis, known as the conscription crisis of 1917, led to a division of the country along language lines; in that year's federal election, every riding where French was the majority language returned an Opposition member.

The second crisis, during World War II, closely resembled the first; it is known as the conscription crisis of 1942. The government put the question of conscription for military service abroad to the voters in a plebiscite; the proposition was defeated almost unanimously in French-speaking Quebec while it received an overwhelming majority in English-speaking Canada. The third crisis occurred in the 1960s, lasted several years, and led to the use of the armed forces in Quebec during the fall of 1970. This third and last crisis was a general opposition to the use of English in Quebec, focussing on the federal public service, crown corporations, banks and financial institutions. One expression of this opposition was the resort to violence, as bombings became a frequent occurrence. The electoral success of the Parti Québécois is in fact an aftermath of the crisis of the late 1960s.

French Canadians who fight for their language do so for many reasons. Some of these reasons relate to individual and group psychology, others to sociology, and still others to economics. Psychology teaches us that individuals value highly their own characteristics and their particular surroundings, which they know best and find reassuring. Conversely they tend to avoid people who exhibit different characteristics and they feel insecure when they find themselves in unfamiliar surroundings. A child learns at a very early age to identify with his social surroundings. He is taught to seek out other individuals who share the same language and the same values with him and to avoid encounters with aliens, outsiders, people who speak differently and profess different values. The learning and socialization process generally accentuates attitudes which lead individuals to associate with other individuals who show similar characteristics, and to reject those who appear different.

Naturally, French-speaking Canadians tend to associate with individuals who speak French and who profess their values, just as English-speaking Canadians tend to associate with other English-speaking Canadians. As a consequence of such natural tendencies, members of the two main linguistic groups of Canada usually locate in different territories, or in different wards or neighborhoods. Normally they do not intermarry. When time comes to find a job, to rent an apartment or to buy a house, the choice is simple: people who go where members of their group dominate can find a normal and socially rewarding existence; those who move where members of the other group dominate find themselves in the situation of any immigrant thrown into new, unfamiliar and largely hostile social surroundings. French Canadians who move "west" find themselves confronted with the terrible choice faced by immigrants everywhere: either they try to adopt the language and values of the majority with the hope of becoming part of it or they stick to their own traditional manners, language and values and remain "outsiders".

There is no joy in being an immigrant. An immigrant has to face considerable problems. He is alone, isolated, segregated, or, at best, linked with other immigrants who are segregated as a group. Like a child, an immigrant has to learn a language, a whole system of values, and social manners. An immigrant has to build a new network of personal relationships: he has no relatives in his new surroundings, no old friends. People migrate for various reasons, but usually they only do so if the benefits of moving outside their familiar surroundings outweigh the costs of such a move.

French Canadians who fight for their language do so because they do not want to become immigrants in their homeland. The politics of English unilingualism in Canada have already made "immigrants" of French Canadians born outside Quebec. Many French Canadians in Quebec are determined to avoid such a fate in the only province where, so far, their language has not been seriously threatened. That is the primary reason why so many French Canadians fight to preserve the French language; they want to retain the language and the set of values they acquired in childhood. Many French Canadians, like many people everywhere, object to the idea of learning two languages and two sets of values, when only one should suffice. Why should they expend their energies learning a second language when they already lack the time, money and energy needed to acquire technical skills that could equip them for productive roles in their society?

In spite of their objection to the idea of learning a second language, many French Quebecers have been forced to do so in order to find a job in their own province, because the managers of Canadian corporations have generally insisted that their employees be able to speak English, wheher or not English is actually used on the job. By the 1960s, this situation had been maintained for such a long time that a large proportion of French-speaking Canadians were convinced that "bilingualism" was highly desirable.*

The Economics and Politics of Bilingualism

The greatest enthusiasm for bilingualism can be found among intermediaries between French-speaking and English-speaking Canadians: bilingual salesmen, bilingual managers, bilingual advertisers, and so on. They support the politics of bilingualism in Canada and, notably, the idea of a bilingual federal public service and bilingual districts. When the pressures for French unilingualism in Quebec, culminating in the proposal to create a separate Republic of Quebec, reached the boiling point in the early 1960s, the promoters of bilingualism found unexpected allies. Those who were afraid of the prospects of the partition of the country joined the linguistic minorities of the various provinces in support of the bilingualization of Canada. The idea was seen as a solution to the language problem of the country.

The federal government declared French and English the official languages of Canada. Zones where French-speaking and English-speaking Canadians coexist in substantial proportions were declared "bilingual districts". The program aimed at making federal services available in both languages in the bilingual districts and providing a

* According to a survey conducted by the Groupe de Recherches Sociales in 1965, more than 90 per cent of the French-speaking respondents were in favor of "bilingualism" (Report of the Royal Commission on Bilingualism and Biculturalism [Ottawa: Queen's Printer, 1967], pages 97, 135).

French-language working milieu for French-speaking federal employees. The federal government provided new resources for the minorities in the bilingual districts, with the objective of ensuring their survival. In the recruitment and career planning of federal government employees, special care was given to improving the proportion of the French-speaking population in the civil service.

Between 1964 and 1974, Quebec, Ontario and New Brunswick all took measures to promote the French language. In Quebec, the provincial government of Liberal Premier Robert Bourassa declared French the leading language of Quebec, English remaining the language of the minority. The English-speaking Quebec minority obtained formal guarantees concerning education in English for children born into families where English was in common use. At the same time, in Ontario and New Brunswick, the French-speaking minorities were offered better services and new language guarantees. Both the Acadians of New Brunswick (200,000 in a population of 634,000) and the Franco-Ontarians (325,000 in a population of 7,700,000) had fought a long battle for such guarantees.

These federal and provincial measures stirred a lot of interest but they did not achieve what they were meant to. They did not stop the growth of the movement for French unilingualism in Quebec, though they did tend to foster some anti-French or anti-Quebec feelings all over Canada (as revealed by the Goldfarb survey published in September 1977 in the Southam papers, and as documented in Jean Bériault's book, *Anti-Québec*). These measures did not stop the growth of Quebec independence parties and did not stop the process of assimilation of French Canadians in the "bilingual districts" outside Quebec. But millions of dollars have been poured into language training, bilingual advertising, translation, and so on.* The main beneficiaries of bilingualism seem to be those who were bilingual already.

In 1971, 13.4 per cent of the entire population of Canada was said to be bilingual in French and English: out of 21,568,000 Canadians registered by the 1971 census, 2,900,000 said they were "able to speak both English and French." Of these, 1,664,000 lived in Quebec,

---

* In his *Fifth Annual Report* (1975), the Commissioner of Official Languages (Ottawa) revealed that, between 1964 and 1974, 58,000 federal public servants (about 50,000 of them were Anglophones) had received free language training during working hours (page 3). However, scarcely 11 per cent of English-speaking public servants taking Language Bureau courses attained standard 1, which constitutes really functional bilingualism (page 6). Moreover, only five per cent of

716,000 in Ontario, 207,000 in the Atlantic provinces and 312,000 in western Canada. In Quebec, 632,000 people said they spoke English only, 3,668,000 said they spoke French only, 63,000 said they spoke neither French nor English, and 1,664,000 were bilingual (27.6 per cent of the total of 6,027,000 Quebecers). Among the bilingual Quebecers, fewer than 20 per cent were of non-French origin.

Outside Quebec, among the 1,235,000 bilinguals, 713,000 said their mother tongue was French. In New Brunswick, 98,000 bilinguals had French as their mother tongue, while 101,000 French-speaking New Brunswick Acadians said that they spoke no English. In Ontario, 260,000 bilinguals had French as their mother tongue. Only 93,000 out of the 353,000 Ontarians who had French as their mother tongue said they spoke only French (in other words, only 25 per cent of Franco-Ontarians were unilingual). In western Canada, those who speak French and English are usually people of French origin. Except for children, people of French origin living in western Canada speak English. Among the 15 million Canadians of other than French origin living outside Quebec, only 3.6 per cent—the vast majority of them in Ontario—said in 1971 that they spoke both French and English. Many French-speaking Quebecers have opposed the bilingualization scheme, arguing that it would only lead to the increased minoritization of French-speaking Canadians. Such positions have been held with consistent vigor by the largest patriotic organizations in Quebec, the St.-Jean-Baptiste Society of Montreal and the Mouvement Québec Français.

The Crisis of Canadian Identity

French Canadians active in federal politics adhere to the idea that their country is the whole of Canada, the territory extending from the Atlantic Ocean to the Pacific. They believe that Canada is the common country of two large language groups, with the French-speaking group concentrated in Quebec but not limited to it. Many of them would like to see the federal civil service staffed by French-speaking Canadians roughly in proportion to their percentage in the population

Anglophone language course graduates make "extensive" use of their acquired French at work (page 8). About three per cent of Francophone federal employees in Quebec were still forced in 1975 to work in English, in Quebec (page 13). The 1,400 translators of the federal government translation bureau are expected to cost $60 million in 1980 (page 19).

as a whole, and to obtain service in French from government offices and government-owned airlines, railways and hotels all across Canada. This is one view of what is or what should be the country called Canada, and it has been the dominant one in the federal government since the mid-1960s.

There is also a second view, which had been latent for a long time and which has been growing in support in Quebec since the mid-1960s. According to this view, first popularized by the former Rassemblement pour l'Indépendance Nationale,* French-speaking Canadians are "foreigners" in the provinces of Canada where English-speaking Canadians constitute a majority. In other words, Quebec is the only territory which French-speaking Canadians can rightly call their country. In matters of language, according to this view, the provinces other than Quebec have shown their refusal to accept linguistic minorities by 100 years of efforts to "assimilate" their French-speaking inhabitants. And the assimilation process in the other provinces has been a success (except in border areas such as eastern Ontario and northern New Brunswick). Outside Quebec, according to the 1971 census, 1,421,000 Canadians were of French origin, but among them only 926,000 declared French as their mother tongue, and only 676,000 said that they usually spoke French at home. The assimilation of French-speaking minorities outside Quebec has been under way for such a long time that there is no reason to expect things will change because the federal government has enacted language legislation favoring French. Accordingly, the argument runs, French-speaking Canadians should abandon any dream of a bilingual Canada; they should, on the contrary, concentrate their efforts on building a French unilingual Quebec, and forget about Canada. In this perspective, French Quebec should behave toward its English-speaking minority just as other Canadian provinces have behaved toward their French-speaking minorities.

These two main views constitute the extreme political alternatives confronting contemporary Quebec: a more or less unilingual Quebec within a formally bilingual Canada, or a rather unilingual Quebec, separate from but associated with a rather unilingual English Canada. There are, of course, other options: assimilation of the 5,500,000 French Canadians to the 250,000,000-strong English-speaking North

---

* Party led by Pierre Bourgault in the 1966 Quebec election. It got approximately 5.6 per cent of the vote, and later dissolved so that its members could join the Parti Québécois.

American "society" is one such option. The bilingualization of Quebec is another. But these other options are not supported by any political party in Quebec and do not appear to appeal to any substantial number of French-speaking Quebecers. On the language question, French-speaking Quebecers share a consensus on the following basic objective: French should be safeguarded, and it should be the dominant language of Quebec. In other words, French Canadians generally agree on the objective of making French the only language required of French Canadians in Quebec.

However, even if a majority of them agree on this basic objective, French Canadians are still divided on some aspects of the language question. Some, such as Bernard Smith, would like to see the "privileged status of the English language abolished".[1] Others, such as Claude Ryan of *Le Devoir*, insist on the rights of the English-speaking minority of Quebec.[2] Raymond Barbeau articulates the most distant possibility: "There is no hope for French-Canadian minorities but from an independent Quebec which would obtain for French-Canadian minorities the same rights that are awarded to Quebec English-speaking minorities."[3]

The Idea of a French-Speaking Quebec People

With the exception of border regions and the western half of Montreal Island, the whole territory of Quebec is in some ways already unilingual and French. In virtually every region of Quebec except for Montreal and the border fringe, the proportion of French-speaking Quebecers in the total regional population runs in the 95 per cent range.* In Metropolitan Montreal, where half the population of Quebec is now concentrated, this proportion is only 66 per cent. English-speaking Quebecers live in Montreal or in areas bordering Ontario or the United States. In similar fashion, French-speaking Canadians living outside Quebec are concentrated in areas bordering Quebec (eastern Ontario and northern New Brunswick).

Quebec is as unilingual and French as the whole of Canada is unilingual and English. The zones where there are substantial linguistic minorities are delineated on the accompanying map. These zones

* Statistics Canada, Catalogue 92-758, *Population by Mother Tongue.* Among these "all-French" districts: Bagot, Beauce, Beauharnois, Bellechasse, Berthier, Champlain, Charlevoix, Chicoutimi, Dorchester and Drummond.

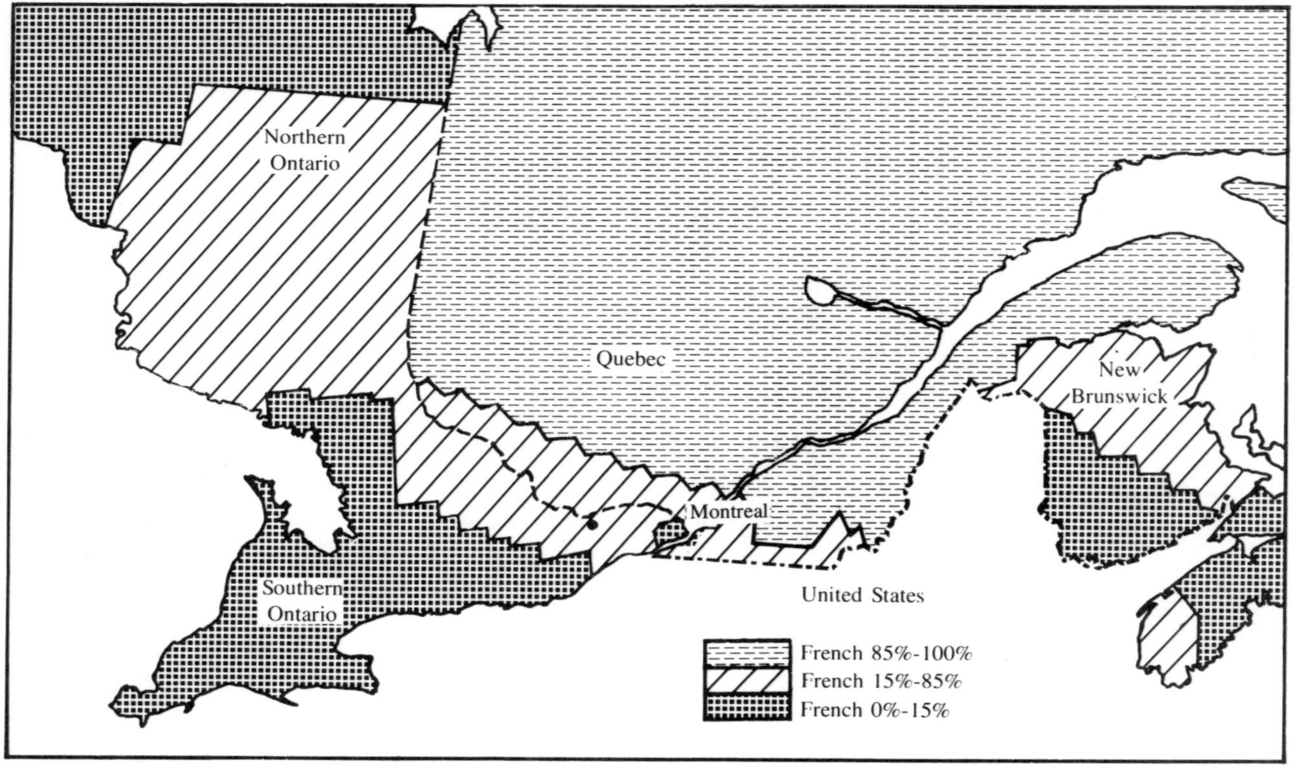

Figure 2 The French Language Territory

Legend:

- French 85%-100%
- French 15%-85%
- French 0%-15%

Northern Ontario

Southern Ontario

Quebec

Montreal

New Brunswick

United States

largely coincide with the so-called bilingual districts defined by the federal government in the early 1970s.

According to surveys conducted in 1971 for Quebec's Gendron Commission on the French language, 86 per cent of the French-speaking population of Quebec experiences a situation of French unilingualism. Of the 4,870,000 French-speaking Quebecers registered in the 1971 census 4,200,000 were living in all-French surroundings. A reading of census data shows that some 3,000,000 French-speaking Quebecers live in areas where English is barely spoken at all, the local population being French in a proportion of 95 per cent or more. Only 39 per cent of Quebecers of French origin say they can speak English. A disproportionate number of these bilingual Quebecers, however, are in the labor force.

The extent of French unilingualism in Quebec largely explains why the "rights" of the English-speaking minority in Quebec hold little direct interest for French-speaking Quebecers, who associate primarily with other French-speaking Quebecers, at home, at play, and at work. From this viewpoint, what is happening in Quebec is similar to what happened in other provinces of Canada when the French-speaking minorities of those provinces were deprived of their language and education "rights".

If the idea of curbing the "rights" of the English-speaking minority in Quebec has not yet obtained the sanction of any political party, the idea of extending the use of French is on the political platform of each of the six major provincial parties of Quebec. And extending the use of French in Quebec generally means making it "attractive" for as many people as possible without encroaching on the constitutional guarantees included in the British North America Act of 1867: the maintenance of denominational schools, a fair parliamentary representation, and the free use of English in the Quebec legislature and in Quebec courts. Yet, as exemplified in the debates surrounding the controversial 1977 Quebec language legislation, variously known as Bill One or Bill 101,* many Parti Québécois activists would like to go as far as possible.

According to another survey conducted for the Gendron Commis-

---

* This bill is now law, and is titled "Charte de la langue française au Québec" (Charter of the French Language in Quebec). It can be obtained from the Editeur Officiel du Québec. Hôtel du Gouvernement, Québec, Québec G1A 1A7.

sion in 1971, nine French-speaking Quebecers out of ten are ready to support government action in favor of French. The survey data showed that 88 per cent of the French-speaking Quebecers interviewed said that they supported such action in one or more areas of interest, such as advertising, communications, language of work, immigration, education, the civil service, textbook publishing and sales, and labelling and marketing practices. And 69 per cent favored action in all or all but one of these eight sectors. The support for government action in favor of French results largely from the idea that French-speaking Quebecers can become a minority if immigrants to Quebec continue to join the English-speaking community.*

But this support for government action in favor of French also results from increased contact between French- and English-speaking people in Quebec. These contacts have affected a growing proportion of the Quebec population since World War II. Before the war, less than 25 per cent of the French-speaking population of Quebec was living in Montreal, where the English-speaking population was concentrated. Outside Montreal, contacts between members of the two linguistic groups were both rare and superficial, just as they are today. On the whole, those who had to complain of regular difficulties with members of the other group were not very numerous. According to the census of 1941, fewer than 20 per cent of the English-speaking inhabitants of Quebec could speak French; indeed 14.6 per cent of the Quebec population of 1941 spoke "English only". By the same token, fewer than 20 per cent of the French-speaking inhabitants of Quebec knew English. The war years, and the industrialization and urbanization that followed, changed this state of affairs. By 1961, more than 30 per cent of Quebec's French-speaking population was concentrated in Montreal, and the percentage of bilingualism had risen to 25 per cent. In 1971, 37 per cent of Quebec's French-speaking population lived in the Montreal area; 27 per cent of all Quebecers were bilingual; and only ten per cent of the Quebec population spoke "English only".

The contacts between the two linguistic groups occur primarily at work. Otherwise the two communities remain largely segregated, with English-speaking Montrealers living on the western half of the island and leaving the eastern part to the French. But in the work area contact is inevitable because the leading employers in the Montreal

---

* This idea is discussed below.

area are large corporations owned by Americans or English-speaking Canadians and managed by English-speaking executives. For as long as anyone can remember, approximately two thirds of the private sector jobs offered in the Montreal area have had "knowledge of English" as a basic requirement.

According to the 1971 surveys already quoted, of 1,163,000 jobs registered in Montreal, 70 per cent required knowledge of the English language. In the rest of Quebec, English was a requirement for fewer than 25 per cent of the jobs registered. In Montreal, according to the same set of data, 46 per cent of the French-speaking people surveyed had obtained their first jobs in positions where English was required.

Many French-speaking Quebecers who need English in order to get or to hold their jobs believe that English is imposed on them by the management, not by the requirements of the job. Indeed, a majority of the French-speaking Quebecers employed in corporations managed by English-speaking executives do in fact work in French, but they have to speak English with managers, engineers, accountants, foremen and salesmen—and they have to read and write English to understand the written instructions prepared by the English-speaking staff or to be understood when reporting to superiors. Many of the 600,000 French-speaking Quebecers who "need" English on the job do not understand why they have to learn a second language, while some 60,000 English-speaking executives and professionals need one language only. In the view of the Mouvement Quebec Français, it would be much easier and more economical to teach a second language to 60,000 managers, executives and professionals than to 600,000 laborers, welders, electricians and other hourly-paid workers. It would be easier still to hire or promote 60,000 French-speaking Quebecers to executive jobs, and to move outside Quebec the 60,000 unilingual English-speaking executives who, according to some Parti Québécois activists, have led Canada into its present state of crisis.

In the view of these activists, this is the nub of the language problem: the owners and managers of large Canadian and American corporations would rather force hourly-paid workers to learn English than promote French Canadians who dare use their own mother tongue. The argument of these activists is strengthened by the fact that the English-speaking "elite" in the Quebec work force has stubbornly held onto English, as shown by the following data taken from the report of the Gendron Commission.

Table 2—Percentage of the Quebec Work Force Showing a High Degree of Fluency in the Other Official Language, by Educational Level and by Mother Tongue

Years of Schooling	French-speaking people Fluent in English	English-speaking people Fluent in French
0 to 8 years	7.6%	16.0%
9 to 11 years	19.6%	12.0%
12 to 14 years	29.8%	12.3%
15 to 16 years	35.9%	10.5%
17 years or more	35.5%	7.3%

Example: line one, column one (7.6%) means that among the French-speaking workers in Quebec who completed between 0 and 8 years of schooling, 7.6% are highly fluent in English.

Source: *Rapport de la Commission d'enquête sur la situation de la langue française et sur les droits linguistiques au Québec* (Gendron Commission— Québec: Editeur Officiel, 1973), table 1.59.

From the viewpoint of the whole society, it would be economically rational for the minority to learn a second language where and when a second language is required. From this perspective, in Quebec corporations bilingualism should be required of the top management, not of the million-strong work force over which the top management presides.

But in spite of the economic rationality behind the movement for a French Quebec, the idea of French unilingualism in Quebec is not without its problems. The first question relates to the proportion of the Quebec population made up of unilingual English-speaking people. Population data show that among the 6,027,000 Quebecers registered in the 1971 census, 13 per cent (789,000) had English as their mother tongue and six per cent (371,000) listed their mother tongue as neither English nor French. Among these 1,160,000 people, 696,000 said that they spoke no French. These 696,000 people account for less than eleven per cent of the total Quebec population, but although this is a lower percentage than the 15 per cent registered in 1941, the problem remains: how is it possible to convert such numbers to the idea of French unilingualism? How can French Quebec teach French to 696,000 unilingual English-speaking people when English Canada has been unable to teach English to 300,000 unilingual French Canadians living in northern New Brunswick and eastern Ontario?

The second problem posed by the idea of French unilingualism in Quebec relates to structures of employment. What would happen to Quebec corporations if French were forced upon their managers? About 70 per cent of the private-sector jobs available in Montreal are provided by corporations owned and operated by English-speaking people. Moreover many of the corporations owned by French Canadians are suppliers to larger Canadian or American companies. Would there be a tendency for these companies to move their managers out of Quebec, leaving only plant, warehouses, retail stores and terminals? Since the early 1960s, when Quebec's language conflicts started, a number of larger corporations have done just that. Head offices which were located in Montreal have been moved to Toronto, along with accounting, planning, research and other staff services. Further expansion in Quebec has generally been stalled or delayed. Some of these moves and delays have little to do with language conflicts but reflect the general displacement of the economic and demographic centre of gravity in North America from east to west. Nevertheless the problem is real.

And what would happen to all the English-speaking workers who work in Quebec without knowing French? In 1971, out of a work force of 2,340,000 people, 521,000 Quebec workers had a mother tongue other than French. Among these 521,000 only 224,000 needed French regularly on their jobs. What will happen to the unilingual English-speaking Quebecers if the English-speaking managers move out of Quebec, taking most administrative functions with them and leaving behind nothing but the production and distribution facilities, which are already staffed by French-speaking employees? These problems are accentuated by the fact that most of the 696,000 English-speaking Quebecers who do not speak French and most of the jobs for which French is not a requirement are concentrated in one particular area of Quebec: the western half of the island of Montreal. How will these English-speaking Canadians living in Montreal, many of them well-to-do, react to what they perceive as a threat to themselves?

Awareness of the problems it would cause English-speaking people in Quebec does not stop the idea of a unilingual French-speaking

Quebec from gaining support. French-speaking Quebecers already see benefits for themselves in the government actions that have been taken in favor of French. Although the percentage they constitute in the total personnel of large corporations and institutions has not changed significantly in the last ten to fifteen years, French Canadians have apparently gained easier access to higher levels of management. Moreover, the pressure exerted in favor of English-speaking managers has been reduced. That probably explains why the increase in bilingualism among French-speaking Quebecers, which had been dramatic between 1941 and 1967, was very moderate between 1961 and 1971 and practically nil between 1971 and 1976.

The support given to the idea of French unilingualism in Quebec is partly explained by economic motives on the part of some French-speaking Quebecers. The first beneficiaries of such a change would be the members of Quebec's French-speaking elite. These people have much to gain economically, because recruitment for managerial functions would be restricted to people speaking French. But the extension of French is a matter of material well-being for other French Canadians as well. Many Quebecers believe that the leaders of a group tend to recruit members of their own group when there is a job to fill, and indeed to favor members of their own group in everything they do. If, thanks to language legislation, the French-speaking Quebec elite is able to displace the current English-speaking managers of Quebec's larger corporations, then hundreds of thousands of French-speaking Quebec workers could benefit from this extension of the French language. Instructions will be issued in French, reports will be written in French, managers will speak French, and workers will be able to use differently (through additional technical training or greater leisure) the time, money and energy they now spend on a second language.

The Ideology of National Survival

The idea of a French unilingual Quebec does not rest solely on economic motives or group selfishness. It is also, and probably more significantly, a reflection of the ideology of national survival, which is a dominant feature of social thinking in French Canada. It is based on the belief that French Canadians constitute a *nation*, but a nation which does not control all of the economic and political institutions operating in its territory. It is also based on the belief that the French-Canadian nation is threatened by "outsiders" who control those institutions which, although they operate in French-Canadian territory, are not French-Canadian. And finally, the ideology of national survival prescribes specific goals: the protection of the French-Canadian population and territory and the gradual accession by French Canadians to control over the economic and political institutions which remain outside their command.

The French-Canadian nation, as defined by its leading nationalist thinkers such as Lionel Groulx,* has always been characterized by two fundamental features: the French language and the territory populated by "les Canadiens" ever since the early stages of the European colonization of North America. Although a precise delineation of the French-Canadian territory has never been possible or necessary, French-Canadian nationalist thinkers have shown a very high degree of agreement in their definition of the French-Canadian nation, its problems and its objectives. Their definitions have been modified gradually under the pressure of changing times and conditions, and secondary elements in these definitions have often been presented differently by different social thinkers, but despite these differences of emphasis or detail there has been general agreement on the essentials.

One of the areas of agreement relates to the belief that French Canadians do constitute a nation, separate and distinct from the English-speaking communities of Canada. Indeed French Canadians share a number of characteristics which clearly distinguish their nation in North America: they all speak French; they have with rare exceptions been brought up in the Roman Catholic faith; they can trace their "Canadian" ancestry back to the seventeenth or early eighteenth century. French Canadians generally believe that "their land" was opened by their forefathers long before the arrival of the first British

* Groulx's ideas are well summarized in the following quotation, taken from Ramsay Cook's anthology, *French-Canadian Nationalism* (Toronto: Macmillan of Canada, 1969) page 193:

But in the large country [Canada], we in Quebec have a smaller country, our French province. The land between Montreal and Tadoussac was, for a long time, the cradle and hearthstone of our race. And in this space, more or less, we were confined after the Conquest; on this territory we lived, suffered, grew, we developed our institutions and our ethnic character. Here, in a word, we placed forever our French imprint. And it is the autonomy of this State as well as its national particularism that was recognized in the federal pact of 1867. What is there still lacking for us to feel attached to this land and to determine to stay here at home?

settlers, and they consider that "their territory" is theirs as a heritage: they share a common territory. French Canadians who live in Quebec control social institutions such as the Church, the schools and the media which operate within their territory and affect its population. They also control Quebec provincial and municipal politics. Except for their lack of control over part of their economy and over federal political institutions, French Canadians present, as a group, the usual features which define nations. But, above all, most of them share a common will to survive and a common faith in their future as a nation.

Reading nationalist literature, one discovers that part of the argument revolves around the idea of a conflict of interests between French Canadians and outside groups that threaten the national integrity of the French Canadian people. Some see Quebec as a colony of Canada or the United States.[4] Outside groups, according to this view, covet the territory and the natural resources of Quebec, and they try to exploit French-Canadian manpower to their own selfish ends. In this perspective, these groups constitute a threat to French Canadians; moreover, the actions of these outside groups explain the problems and the economic and political dependency of the French-Canadian people.

Although they generally agree on the existence of an external threat, French-Canadian nationalists are not at all unanimous in defining its nature and origins. Various hypotheses have been proposed by different groups at different times. During the 1950s, when worldwide attention turned on Moscow's Communists, some Quebec nationalists found a threat to their nation in Moscow.* Present-day worldwide anti-Americanism has some echoes in Quebec nationalist circles.** However, a survey of nationalist literature reveals that one group has always been perceived as threatening: the English-speaking magnates of Canadian finance and industry and the bureaucrats of the federal government who are regarded as their servants.

What is perceived as a threat does not necessarily need to be one in

* The leader of the Union Nationale, Premier Maurice Duplessis, became famous in the 1950s for his crusade against Communists. See Herbert Quinn, *The Union Nationale, A Study in Nationalism* (Toronto: University of Toronto Press, 1963).

** The Confederation of National Trade Unions' 1971 pamphlets, *Ne comptons que sur nos propres moyens*, and *Ce n'est qu'un commencement*, illustrate these views.

fact. It would be very difficult to convince Soviet or American diplomats that their country threatens French in Canada, or to convince Toronto financiers or Ottawa civil servants that they constitute a menace to French Canadians. However, French-Canadian nationalists have always been able to support their assertions with examples taken from the news headlines. In 1976, they quoted the opposition to the use of French in air traffic over Quebec, the booing of announcements in French at a hockey game in Toronto, the statistics on immigration, on trade, on investment, on income, on unemployment, on federal spending, and so on.

To resort to the idea of an outside threat to explain one's difficulties is not peculiar to French-Canadian nationalists. This is a common feature of many ideologies, and is held to with equal fervor by trade unions, professional associations, and nations. Social groups usually explain their difficulties by having recourse to some external "cause", be it exploitation of a ruling class, the oppression of a dominant nation, or some combination of the two. When a social group uses an external threat to explain its problems, it also judges its own success by its ability to resist the threat. And this, in French Canada, is another area of agreement. In the view of many Quebec nationalists, the survival of French Canada is not a miracle, it is a feat explained primarily by the solid social virtues of French Canadians and by their veneration of the French language.

The French language, as we have seen, is a fundamental characteristic of the French-Canadian nation, but it is also more than that. It is the symbol of identity for French Canadians as a group, the rallying force among them, their pride and their wealth. It has an appeal which compares to no other group characteristic. In the last analysis, it is what French Canadians fight for. In this light, the idea of a unilingual French-speaking people in the territory populated and dominated by French Canadians is more a reflection of ideology than a formula prompted by narrow economic interests.

The Survival of a French Nation in North America

With rare exceptions, French Canadians are united behind the objective of preserving and extending the use of the French language in the territory where they are numerically dominant. They are also more or less unanimously in favor of defining French Canadians as a nation. And there can be no doubt that French-speaking Canadians agree on the objective of national survival, the survival of a French "nation" in North America.

Among the important questions on which they do not agree is the issue of "rights" to be guaranteed to the English-speaking minority of Quebec. The degree of economic and political subordination consistent with the objective of national survival in an industrialized and highly interdependent world is another area of disagreement, although French Canadians generally believe that the current degree of subordination is too high and should be reduced. Many members of the Parti Québécois believe that the maximum degree of subordination consistent with the survival of the French-Canadian nation is that which would remain after the government of Quebec gained full political sovereignty. However, some Parti Québécois members, and many activists who work with small Marxist organizations, believe that formal political sovereignty is not enough. Others, including most members of the opposition parties, believe that full sovereignty is much more than what is required.

Those who oppose the objective of Quebec political sovereignty generally argue against it on the grounds that it would endanger the very French-Canadian nation that it is meant to protect. They oppose the reduction of French territory to the limits of Quebec, since such a reduction would spell the end of French-speaking minorities outside Quebec. But, as we have already seen, many French-speaking Quebecers consider that the isolation and level of assimilation of the French-speaking minorities outside Quebec have severed them from the French-Canadian nation. For many members of the Parti Québécois, the French-Canadian nation is now reduced to the territory of Quebec and the adjacent French-speaking "bilingual" districts of northern New Brunswick and eastern Ontario (see figure 2).

A number of French-speaking Canadians, most notably Prime Minister Pierre Trudeau, oppose "nationalism" or, more precisely, French-Canadian nationalism.* However, even among these anti-nationalists, a great many approve of *la survivance française*; they approve of the idea of protecting the French language in Canada, but they condemn French unilingualism and Quebec "separatism". Whatever their position on questions such as bilingualism and English "rights" in Quebec, French Canadians of Quebec are clearly in favor of one common

---

* This anti-nationalism is particularly well expressed in a famous article by Pierre Trudeau, "New Treason of the Intellectuals" in *Federalism and the French Canadians* (Toronto: Macmillan, 1968), pages 151-181.

fundamental objective, *la survivance française*. The survival of the French language is, in the view of a large majority, inseparable from the survival of a French-speaking nation in North America.

2

Economic Well-Being

Like national survival, economic progress is an objective on which French-Canadian political leaders agree. But while some leaders are careful not to talk about the French-Canadian "nation" when they address themselves to English-speaking audiences, no leader would hesitate to voice his faith in economic progress.

The economic complaints heard in Quebec often seem more pressing than those which are heard in other parts of Canada. Quebec has been lagging behind the Canadian average per capita income since the end of World War I. Various explanations have been advanced for this lag, and these explanations lead to a variety of proposed solutions, but the objective remains the same: everybody would like to improve the well-being of French-speaking Quebecers.

Quebec's Economic Lag

The national accounts published regularly since 1926 show that the gap between Quebec per capita income and Canadian per capita income has oscillated around an average 15-percentage-point spread. Canadian per capita income being 100, Quebec has usually registered about 85. And a similar discrepancy is found in every standard per capita index of production or consumption.

At the same time, Quebec has been, along with the Atlantic provinces, a leader in unemployment in Canada. The rate of unemployment in Quebec is regularly more than 25 per cent above the Canadian average. When the Canadian rate of unemployment is between seven and eight per cent, Quebec generally has ten per cent. Ontario, on the other hand, registers an unemployment rate somewhat below the Canadian average: when Quebec's unemployment rate is ten per cent, the Ontario rate is between five and seven per cent. The difference between Quebec and Ontario from the viewpoint of unemployment is more dramatic than the difference registered from the viewpoint of per capita income. When Quebec stands at 85 in comparison to the Canadian average of 100 on the index of per capita income, Ontario stands at 110 or more. The two western provinces of Alberta and British Columbia usually fare almost as well as Ontario, while the four eastern provinces, Newfoundland and Prince Edward Island in particular, fare considerably worse than Quebec (see table 3).

Table 3 – Average Per Capita Income by Province, 1956, 1966 and 1975, with 1976 Populations

Province	1976 Population	Per capita income compared with the Canadian average		
		1956	1966	1975
Newfoundland	559,000	56	62	69
Prince Edward	121,000	55	66	68
Nova Scotia	836,000	74	77	79
New Brunswick	692,000	65	72	77
Quebec	6,267,000	86	89	91
Ontario	8,373,000	119	113	110
Manitoba	1,030,000	94	100	97
Saskatchewan	941,000	83	94	102
Alberta	1,850,000	102	103	104
British Columbia	2,502,000	122	111	107
Canada	23,231,000	100	100	100
Canadian average		$1350	$2303	$5838

Source: Statistics Canada, Geographic Distribution of Personal Income, *National Accounts, Income and Expenditure, 1950–1956*, page 38 and *National Income and Expenditure Accounts, 1961–1975*, pages 46-47, catalogue 13-201.

In order to provide Quebecers with public services in the same quantity and quality as the neighboring province of Ontario or state of New York, the Quebec provincial government must resort to higher rates of taxation. Quebec rates for standard taxes run ten to fifteen per cent above the Canadian average. In 1976, a citizen of Quebec earning $25,000 in taxable income was paying $825 more in income taxes than an average fellow Canadian with similar income, and $1,400 more than a $25,000-a-year Albertan.

However, contrary to what one might expect, wages and salaries paid in Quebec compare closely to those paid in Ontario or New York, at least since the mid-1960s. Moreover, minimum wage regulations since the mid-1960s have been more favorable to workers in Quebec than in most Canadian provinces. Taxation statistics published annually by the federal Department of National Revenue reveal that individual incomes by occupational category often reach higher averages in Quebec than in many other provinces. Census data confirm these taxation statistics: in 1971, the average income, for all people *with income*, was $4,969 in Quebec, only $64 less than the average in the country as a whole.

Economic Lag and Demographic Structure

There seems to be a paradox in the fact that the wage paid in Quebec for a specific job to a person with specific credentials is similar to the wage paid in Ontario for the same job, while Quebec's per capita income lags 20 to 30 points behind Ontario's.* The paradox is only apparent, because income statistics are related to the demographic structure of a population, and a significant part of the difference in per capita income between Quebec and Ontario is explained by the demographic structure of Quebec. Because of its traditionally higher birthrate, Quebec has always had a larger percentage of children (under fifteen years of age) than Ontario. In 1971, 4,242,175 Quebecers, or 70 per cent of the total population of 6,027,000, were of

---

* In its study of regional disparities, published in April 1977, the Economic Council of Canada explained that the differences in per capita income between the various provinces of Canada result from differences in productivity from one region to the other. These differences in productivity do not result from differences between "industrial structures" but, in 80 per cent of the cases, from differences in the professional qualifications of manpower. In 1970, for instance, the average Quebec and Atlantic worker had 10 years of schooling, while Alberta and British Columbia workers had 11 years. The lower education level of the Quebec labor force explains four points of an 11 percentage point difference between Quebec production per worker and Ontario production per worker. See *Living Together: A Study of Regional Disparities*, Ottawa, 1977 (catalogue no. EC 22-54/1977).

working age. Ontario, the same year, had 71 per cent of its population of working age (5,495,000 out of 7,703,000). In 1961, the respective proportions were 64 per cent (3,396,000 out of 5,259,000) in Quebec, and 67 per cent (4,228,000 out of 6,236,000) in Ontario. These figures reflect the higher birthrate of Quebec and the higher immigration to Ontario. Up to 1966, for every thousand inhabitants one could find roughly 30 more children in Quebec than in Ontario. Until very recently, Quebec adults had more mouths to feed than Ontario adults: that is one explanation of Quebec's lower income per capita (including adults and children) at least for the period extending to the mid-1960s.

Moreover, the percentage of adults who work outside home for an income has regularly been lower in Quebec than in Ontario. Several factors explain this lower rate of participation in the labor force. One relates to the pressures on many Quebec women to stay home and rear children; the ideal of high fertility and the economic dependency of women were dominant values in French-Canadian society until the mid-1960s. Another reason has been the persistence of seasonal employment practices forced upon Quebec's rural population by climate, geography, and habitat dispersal. Habitat dispersal has hindered manpower mobility and contributed to underemployment in rural areas. These factors and many others, which have little to do with "discrimination", have made for a participation index somewhat lower in Quebec than in Ontario. In 1971, for instance, only 54 per cent of Quebecers aged 15 and over had a paid job or were looking actively for one (2,394,000 out of 4,242,000 adults were in the labor force). In Ontario, the same year, the corresponding proportion was 58 per cent (3,249,000 people in the labor force out of 5,495,000 aged fifteen and over). In 1961, the percentages were 52 per cent in Quebec and 57 per cent in Ontario. In other words, among 1,000 adults, in 1961, 480 stayed home in Quebec, but only 430 in Ontario: a difference of 50, or almost ten per cent. The proportional difference remained roughly the same for decades but it has been declining gradually since the mid-1960s.

A significant part of the Quebec unemployment rate can be explained by demography. Because of Quebec's traditionally higher birthrate, the number of young people looking for a first job has been proportionally higher in Quebec than in Ontario, leading to a higher unemployment rate among Quebec youth. Unemployed Quebec youths (16 to 24 years of age) have sometimes accounted for almost half of Canadian unemployment in this age category. Another demographic factor, which has become significant in the last 15 years, relates to the recent decrease in Quebec's birthrate. While the positive effects of this decrease in terms of youth unemployment will not really be felt until after 1980, the transition has made for another increase in unemployment: a growing proportion of Quebec women are becoming liberated from the traditional obligations of motherhood, and as a consequence, Quebec women are arriving on the labor market in much greater proportions than before, and in greater proportions than Ontario women. This recent phenomenon has led to a very high level of unemployment among Quebec women, who have regularly accounted for some 35 per cent of unemployed Canadian women for the last 10 to 15 years.

The Difference Between Quebec and Ontario

The 1971 24-percentage-point difference between Quebec per capita income ($3,027) and Ontario per capita income ($3,967) is explained by:

A. Demographic factors, for ten percentage points:

In 1971, Quebec had 2,197,000 people employed in a total population of 6,027,000 (36 per cent) and Ontario had 3,079,000 people employed in a total population of 7,703,000 (40 per cent). The difference between 36 and 40 is four, that is ten per cent of 40. This difference results from the fact that Quebec, in 1971, had a greater proportion of young people in its population than Ontario, a lower rate of participation of its women in the labor force, and a greater territorial dispersion of its population.

B. Factors of economic structure for ten percentage points:

One third of these ten percentage points in 1971 was related to the lower education level of the average Quebec worker; another third was a result of the Quebec overrepresentation in the highly competitive textile, clothing and furniture industries; and the last third was related to other structural characteristics of Quebec economy (non-resident ownership of large corporations, for instance).

C. Other factors, including the impact of federal government spending, for four percentage points.

The higher Quebec unemployment rate, which is explained partly by demography, partly by Quebec's adverse climate and seasonal work practices in primary production sectors, partly by rural habitat dispersal, and partly by other factors such as Quebec's industrial structure and dependency on foreign markets, also has a significant bearing on Quebec's per capita production and income. In 1971, for instance, there were on the average 197,000 unemployed in Quebec, while Ontario had only 170,000. In 1961, the numbers were 168,000 (9.3 per cent unemployment rate) in Quebec, and 132,000 (5.5 per cent) in Ontario.

All these demographic factors have their effects on the per capita production and income figures. In 1971, these factors gave Quebec 2,197,000 employed people in a total of 6,027,000 population (36 per cent of the population actually worked). In the same year, Ontario had 3,079,000 people employed (or 40 per cent) in a total population of 7,703,000. Proportionally, the difference between Quebec and Ontario was thus about ten per cent. In 1961, the proportions were 31 per cent (Quebec) and 36 per cent (Ontario). In other words, Quebec's employment as a fraction of the total population is ten to fifteen per cent lower than Ontario's.

In summary, demographic and labor statistics explain a large part of the lower per capita income of Quebec in comparison with Ontario or with Canada as a whole. All other things being equal, up to 1971, the demographic characteristics of Quebec and of Ontario accounted for a ten per cent difference in their per capita income.

Economic Lag and the Structure of Industry

But all other things are not equal: other structural characteristics account for another ten per cent difference in the per capita income of Canada's two largest provinces. These relate to Quebec industry. Quebec is overrepresented in several industrial sectors which are labor-intensive and severely threatened by international competition. Moreover, Quebec's industrial structure is dominated by corporations which are owned by non-residents. As a consequence, per capita capital income is lower in Quebec than in Ontario.

A large part of Quebec's manufacturing sector was developed before 1950: it is now aging, it remains labor-intensive, it is beset with social problems related to technical modernization, and it is adversely affected by the expansion of manufacturing production in newly industrialized countries where wages are considerably lower than in Quebec. This is the case in the textile, clothing, leather, footwear, furniture and electronics sectors, all sectors in which Quebec accounts for a large share (between 30 and 50 per cent) of total Canadian production. Competition from poorer countries leads to underpricing and underpaying, which in turn further delays technical modernization and accentuates social problems such as worker dissatisfaction and strikes.

A significant proportion of the Quebec work force, a larger proportion than in Ontario, is employed in the sectors most affected by obsolescence and international competition. Wages rank well below those paid in sectors such as the automotive industry, where competition comes from fully-developed, high-wage industrial countries. While Quebec suffers from world competition in sectors where world prices are lower than Canadian prices, Ontario benefits from the world price levels established in the industrial sectors in which it is strong (notably the automobile industry), Alberta benefits from world prices in the energy resources which abound in its territory, and British Columbia benefits from the growth of trade among Pacific Rim countries.

Another characteristic of Quebec industry which adversely affects per capita income relates to the ownership of its largest corporations. Just as in Canada as a whole, industry in Quebec is dominated by American multinational corporations, especially those which manufacture such complex products as chemicals, drugs and engines. But unlike Ontario, Quebec has a further absentee ownership problem. A growing proportion of shares in Canadian corporations operating in Quebec have left Quebec and gone to Ontario. Moreover, unlike Ontario, Quebec now clearly falls outside the North American centre of gravity, which has moved from east to west with the passage of time. As a consequence of this general displacement to the west, Canadian capital has tended to leave Quebec in order to remain in the mainstream of North American development. Foreign as well as Canadian investors have naturally favored Ontario or the western provinces because the pace of development held out the promise of higher yields on capital invested there. As the most significant expansion takes place to the west, Quebec is passed by.

As a general consequence of both the non-resident ownership of Quebec's largest corporations and the relatively lower rate of private investment in Quebec, millions of dollars of profits generated by Quebec labor and Quebec consumers are collected and spent or reinvested outside Quebec, south and west of its borders.

Finally, because of their traditionally high birthrate and consequent high level of demographic expenses, the French Canadians of Quebec have not been able to amass much capital. What their thrift has allowed them to save has been primarily channeled into insurance premiums and bonds over which Quebec residents do not exert much control. This capital, owned indirectly by inhabitants of Quebec, has also tended to pull out in order to follow the westward trend. As a result of all this, capital income in Quebec is considerably less than in Ontario.

Altogether, the aging and threatened Quebec manufacturing sector with its low wages and the low capital income registered in Quebec because of the non-resident ownership of its larger corporations account for another ten-percentage-point difference in per capita income between Quebec and Ontario.

Economic Lag and the Cost of Cultural Differentiation

The demographic and structural factors which explain most of the economic lag experienced by Quebec in comparison to Ontario are similar to those which explain the economic lag of the four Atlantic provinces as well as that which affects several of the eastern states in the American federation. But Quebec's economic lag is also partly explained by Quebec cultural differentiation. By maintaining French as their language, French Canadians reduce their territorial mobility and sever themselves from the flow of ideas and innovation which fuels North American economic progress.

Some of the authors of the anti-independence book, *Le séparatisme? Non! 100 fois non!*[5] think that the price paid by French Canadians for their "national survival" is much less than what it would be if Quebec were not subsidized by the rest of Canada and if Quebec industry were not managed by English-speaking Canadians. According to this view, by being part of the Canadian federation, French Canadians benefit from government services that they could not afford if they were left by themselves, and by opening their territory to North American industrialists, French Canadians avoid the disaster that they would face if they had to count on their own elite for innovation and gains in productivity. Indeed, in this perspective, French Canadians should be amply satisfied with their economic and political situation, because by and large they fare a lot better economically than those Canadians who live in the four eastern provinces.

Attempts to explain Quebec's economic lag by such "cultural

causes", are generally bolstered by statistics relating to religion and education, factors which have long differentiated Quebec from the rest of Canada. Taking into account not only language but also religion and education, one can make a very convincing argument for the "cultural explanation" of Quebec's economic lag.

The religious factor is the most obvious. French Canadians, with rare and statistically insignificant exceptions, are all Roman Catholics, while 75 per cent of all English-speaking Canadians are Protestants. The hypothesis is that the Protestant ethic has favored economic progress, industrialization, and capitalism, while these developments are hindered by the Catholic ethic. The demonstration of this hypothesis consists of a comparison between the industrial production of countries where Protestantism dominates and that of countries where Catholicism dominates. There is indeed a correlation: Germany, England, and the United States are all highly industrialized and dominated by Protestants, while Spain, Portugal and the South American republics are much less industrialized and dominated by Catholics. In Canada, the economic elite is dominated by Protestants, who hold about 75 per cent of the executive positions in large Canadian corporations.

The value of the argument must not be exaggerated, however, and one should be cautious when talking of the influence of religion on the economy. Although one can see a correlation between religion and industrial development, it is very difficult to find a *direct* causal relationship between the two. Economic development results from a variety of factors which can be directly related to production, know-how, trade, organization, resources, transportation, climate, technical innovation, and so on; none of these factors is directly related to religion. Moreover, the religious argument obviously does not take into account the changes that have occurred in Quebec since 1960.

Religion has to be mentioned as a factor when one tries to explain Quebec's economic lag, but the hypothesis has yet to be tested conclusively and the part of the economic lag that religion can explain has yet to be measured. Surely, the methodological problems involved in a measure of the influence of religion on the economic development of Quebec would be considerable. But up to the 1960s and perhaps later, the influence of the Roman Catholic Church in Quebec had at least an indirect impact on the economic development of French Canada, through Church influence in matters such as education and birthrate.

The phenomenal birthrate registered by French Canadians, which produced a demographic structure that greatly affected per capita income, was partly a consequence of values nurtured by the Catholic ethic. According to Jacques Henripin, "During the last two centuries, world population has been multiplied by three, European population by four, and French-Canadian population by eighty, in spite of net emigration that can be estimated roughly at 800,000."[6] This is particularly remarkable in light of French-Canadian emigration to the United States: between 1870 and 1930, close to a million French Canadians left Canada to go to the United States; in 1950, 13 million Americans had at least one grandparent born in French Canada; and 2,600,000 Americans spoke French at home in 1970.

The social role of women, as seen by leading members of the Catholic clergy, did not admit of work outside the home. The lower rate of participation of French-Canadian women in the labor force, while partly explained by family responsibilities and lower employment opportunities in rural areas, also has to do with attitudes consonant with the teachings of the clergy. Another area where Church influence has certainly been significant is the "agricultural vocation" of French Canada. From the 1840s to the 1950s, a large segment of the Catholic clergy of Quebec advocated a philosophy of agriculturalism; farming was believed to be the ideal achievement of man on earth. Although these views were challenged by a minority in the clergy, they contributed nevertheless to French Canadians remaining in rural areas, kept them from engaging in industry and influenced school curricula. Birthrate, lower rate of female participation in the work force, and attitudes toward industrialization and education have all had an impact on the economic development of French Canada, and they account for part of Quebec's lower per capita income. However, the influence of the Church in such matters is both indirect and difficult to measure.

Another cultural explanation of Quebec's economic lag relates to levels of education. The fact is that, in 1961, 55 per cent of Quebec adults had seven years or less of schooling, while the comparable figure in Ontario was 45 per cent. It is also a fact that up to the early 1970s, French-speaking universities produced fewer than ten per cent of Canada's graduates in engineering and the sciences, while Quebec French Canadians accounted for 23 per cent of the country's population. Moreover, in fields such as engineering, chemistry and the social sciences, French-Canadian university graduates have long constituted only ten to fifteen per cent of the total Canadian professional membership.

Educational level and personal income correlate within the same age bracket and within the same linguistic groups. But for the same educational level and the same age bracket, there is also a significant "linguistic differential" between French- and English-speaking Canadians in terms of personal income (1961 data), as revealed in the Report of the Royal Commission on Bilingualism and Biculturalism in 1969. One example can illustrate this: upon graduating from university, the "average" English-speaking Canadian, in 1961, was getting $800 more than the "average" French-speaking Canadian. According to the B and B Commission Report, French-speaking Canadians were those who benefited least from their education. Studies based on the 1971 census show that the situation has not changed significantly (see box). However, one should take into account, before concluding that discrimination does exist, that French-Canadian university graduates tend to take the jobs available in their own local communities rather than compete for better-paid jobs available outside.

Some attention could be directed toward the content of school curricula in the French-speaking educational system. Indeed, until the late 1960s, the French-speaking schools of Quebec offered a smaller amount of "technical" instruction than the English-speaking schools of Ontario or other provinces. The differences in the school curricula probably led to differences between graduates of the two main linguistic groups in terms of managerial or technical capabilities. Such differences, in turn, possibly explain differences in personal income at the start of a career. One should talk of "discrimination" only when people with similar credentials are paid different salaries and offered different work conditions because of their ethnic origin, religion, skin color or sex.

According to our analysis, factors related to the French-Canadian culture explain *directly* only a small part of the difference between Quebec and Ontario in terms of per capita income. At best, it is risky to explain the whole of the economic lag which affects Quebec by resorting to nothing but the cultural differentiation hypothesis. Our analysis has shown, so far, that Quebec's economic lag is primarily and directly explained by demographic and structural factors (in 1961, 20 points of the 30-point difference between Quebec and Ontario per capita income were so explained). Our analysis has also shown that one of the cultural factors (education) directly explains approximately

Unilingual Francophones Got Lowest Pay in 1971

Bilingual French-speaking employees earned less than unilingual anglophones in 1971 while unilingual francophones dropped into last place among the province's wage earners, a study published Saturday shows.

The purpose of the study by François Vaillancourt, an economics professor at the University of Montreal, was to update 1961 statistics used by the royal commission on bilingualism and biculturalism, known as the B and B commission.

"The francophone worker is still the most underprivileged, regardless of his occupation, and even if he becomes bilingual he cannot match the anglophone, bilingual or not, except in the case of office employees," said Vaillancourt.

In 1971 the average earnings of a unilingual francophone employee were 64 per cent lower than for a unilingual anglophone. However, the gap between bilingual employees in both groups dropped to 20 per cent in favor of anglophones, the study showed.

With only 14 per cent of the Quebec population, anglophones held 31 per cent of administrative positions and only 10 per cent of production jobs in 1971.

In 1961 francophones were in second-last place in average earnings, just ahead of Italians. Vaillancourt's results showed that between 1961 and 1971, francophones slipped into last place.

Source: *The Gazette*, Montreal, May 2, 1977, page 3.

another five points of this difference. In other words, the "cultural explanation" does account for a part of Quebec's economic lag, but no more.*

Moreover, a survey of the data for the last 25 years also shows that Quebec's economic lag has been reduced gradually as its demographic structure slowly improved in comparison with Ontario's and its educa-

* In 1971, according to the Economic Council of Canada, education and culture accounted for four points in an eleven point difference between Ontario and Quebec income *per worker*. See *Living Together: A Study of Regional Disparities*, Ottawa, 1977 (catalogue no. EC 22-54/1977).

tional system underwent profound changes. In the 1970s, Quebec's birthrate has fallen below the Canadian average, a dramatic change compared with the 1950s. In the 1970s, Quebec school enrolment, at all levels, has become one of the highest in Canada. These changes have been reflected in the economic sphere: the difference between Quebec and Ontario in terms of per capita income has been reduced gradually. This difference was more than 30 points before 1963; it was down to 25 in 1967; in 1977 it oscillated around 20 points.

Our analysis, which is limited to the first level of causal relationships, emphasizes demographic, structural and educational factors. But the analysis could be pushed further: one could try, for instance, to discover what "caused" the Quebec school curriculum of the 1900-1960 period to be what it was. One could also correlate recent changes in the demographic trends and in education with the recent decline of Church influence, or the recent impact of television. But, in every such case, the relationship with Quebec economic performance would be indirect and very difficult to establish precisely. What one can say is that Quebec's economic lag in terms of per capita income is related *directly* to factors such as demography, industrial structures and educational levels, and *indirectly* to such phenomena as ethics, values and culture, as well as to habitat dispersal, climate, natural resources, foreign markets and so on. It would be a gross exaggeration to emphasize a single explanation—the more so if that explanation is not directly verifiable. In short, the cultural differentiation hypothesis does not provide anything resembling a complete explanation of the Quebec economic lag.

The Quebec Business Community

Another aspect of the "cultural differentiation hypothesis" has to do with the proportion of English-speaking people in the Quebec business community. Census statistics reveal that, in the Quebec private sector (which accounts for a little more than 75 per cent of employment in the province), some 60 per cent of the executives are of French origin, while people of French origin make up 82 per cent of the entire population. This imbalance does not apply to public-sector executive positions, including some para-public activities.

Quebecers of an origin other than French register a higher education level than French Canadians, and they have average property incomes much larger than French Canadians. Putting the average income at 100, French Canadians employed in Quebec earn only 95, while Quebecers of non-French origin earn 125: a difference of 30 percentage points. The studies conducted for the Royal Commission on Bilingualism and Biculturalism during the 1960s documented this conclusion with 1961 census data and with special surveys.

Real income of the family, household or single individual	*Proportion of the population in the category*	*Main characteristics of the category*
$100,000 and more	3%	90% English-speaking: large industrialists, financiers and merchants
$20,000 to $100,000	12%	40% English-speaking and 50% bilingual: managers, professionals, businessmen
$7000 to $20,000	30%	20% English-speaking, 20% bilingual and 60% French-speaking: smaller professionals, organized workers, large farmers
$4000 to $7000	35%	5% English-speaking, 30% bilingual and 65% French-speaking: unorganized workers, small farmers
$4000 and less	20%	95% French-speaking: unemployed, welfare recipients, students, pensioners

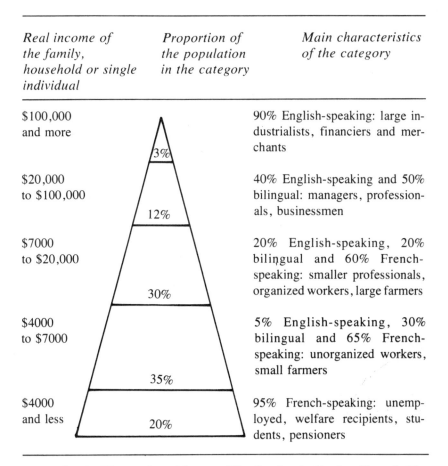

Figure 3   An Illustration of Income Distribution in Quebec Households, 1976

Source: Adaptation, for 1976, of an illustration in Pierre Jauvin, *Le Sous-développement au Québec et dans le monde* (Montreal: Secrétariat national de la Jeunesse ouvrière catholique, 1971).

Note: Pierre Jauvin's table is in turn inspired by a 1969 report of the Quebec Department of Revenue. Income includes capital gains registered in the course of the year.

Taking into account data on earnings, income from property and capital gains, and other data on the number of income-earners per family, one can illustrate income distribution in Quebec (see figure 3).

The Quebec private sector is dominated by a number of large multinational corporations and Canadian-owned banks and trust companies. Although these large firms are few in number, they provide a large proportion of the jobs available and gain a large share of the profits generated in Quebec. These large firms are owned and controlled by outsiders. Quebec's private sector, in the mid-1970s, was made up of some 120,000 firms, including partnerships in the professional sector and individual entrepreneurships. Based on the language used in their communications with the government, some 75 to 80 per cent of these firms were owned by French-speaking individuals. However, fewer than 50 per cent of Quebec workers were employed in these French-speaking firms. And because they were more labor-intensive and concentrated in highly competitive areas, these French-speaking firms produced only 15 per cent of the value-added generated by the Quebec private sector, and a still lower percentage of its profits. Figure 4 indicates that foreign-owned or foreign-controlled firms are those which show by far the best results.

Except for the Banque Canadienne Nationale and the Banque Provinciale, major banks operating in Quebec are owned by English-speaking Canadians. Out of some 1,500 bank branches operating in Quebec in the mid 1970s, only 40 per cent, accounting for some 30 per cent of Quebec's banking business, were branches of French-Canadian banks. The operations of credit unions affiliated with the French-Canadian Mouvement Cooperatif Desjardins only partially offset the imbalance.

According to many French-speaking Canadians, notably Rodrigue Tremblay, Parti Québécois minister of industry, the business practices of English-speaking Quebecers fit the definition of discrimination and of segregation.* One faces discrimination when, within the same territory or firm, the same work and the same work experience command different salaries or work conditions depending on such criteria (acknowledged or not) as sex, race, religion, language or political ideas. In Quebec, according to many, such discrimination exists on all

* Rodrigue Tremblay, preface to a new edition of Errol Bouchette's *L'indépendance économique du Canada français,* (Montréal: La Presse, 1977), p. 28. Errol Bouchette was an economist of the early twentieth century, the first well-known French-Canadian economist.

these bases, and the most widespread discrimination is on the basis of language—against French Canadians. Moreover it is fairly apparent that segregation also prevails. One sees economic segregation when, within the same territory, employees of one particular language, race, or religion are under-represented in firms owned by individuals of another language, race, or religion. In the 1960s, protest against discrimination and segregation reached a boiling point in Quebec.

It is, however, very difficult to link discrimination or segregation to Quebec's economic lag. Linguistic discrimination or segregation does not account for much in a statistical explanation of Quebec's economic lag. But discrimination is thought to exist and it thus explains the difference in perspective between French-speaking Quebecers and

---

Distribution of Quebec private sector employment according to the language and residence of firm owners

Distribution of Quebec private sector generated value-added according to the language and residence of firm owners

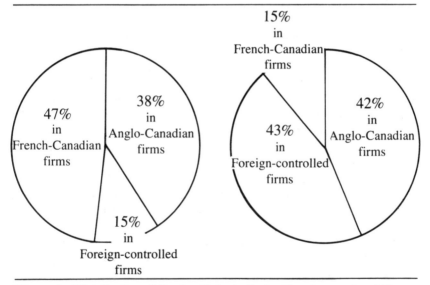

Figure 4   Distribution of Quebec Private Sector Employment and Generated Value-Added, According to the Language and Residence of Firm Owners, mid 1970s

Source: Quebec Department of Industry and Commerce

English-speaking Quebecers. And consequently, it does help account for the electoral success of the Parti Québécois. Indeed, in speaking of discrimination, Rodrigue Tremblay was expressing a widespread French-Canadian belief: many French-Canadians know of relatives and friends who have been fired for their insistence on using French at work, who cannot get jobs because they do not speak English, who have experienced bankruptcy at the hands of English-speaking businessmen. Naturally, when one tries to explain Quebec's economic problems, one resorts to what one knows on the subject, and what one knows best are the statistics of personal experience.

Economic Lag and the Federal Government

Personal experience tells many Quebecers that the federal government has long been another English-speaking employer, "discriminating against French Canadians". From the 1920s to the 1960s, the percentage of French-speaking Quebecers in the federal public service and federal crown corporations remained approximately 15 per cent. Yet French-speaking Quebecers were 23 per cent of the total population of Canada, and French-speaking Canadians, 27 per cent.

Since the mid-1960s, dramatic changes have occurred: the proportion of French-speaking Canadians in the federal public service has grown steadily. In less than ten years, the proportion has grown to 26 per cent (from a low of 12 per cent in 1967). In the "officer categories" (the top tenth of the public service), the proportion of French-speaking Canadians reached 19 per cent in 1976, from 13 per cent in 1971 and 10 per cent in 1966. In the armed forces, the proportion reached 23 per cent in 1976, from 18 per cent in 1971 and 13 per cent in 1961.* In spite of the changes of the last ten years, Quebec nation-

---

* As of April 1, 1977, these were the facts: in Canada, there were 256,206 federal employees covered by the Public Service Commission (this includes approximately 60 departments and agencies out of 120, the main exceptions being the armed forces, Air Canada and the CNR). Out of these 256,206 employees, 69,191 were people who identify themselves as Francophones rather than Anglophones.

Among these 256,206 federal employees, 73,547 were stationed in the national capital region (and of these 23,876 were Francophones). Among these 256,206 federal employees, another 44,230 were stationed in Quebec (Ottawa-Hull excluded) and 40,793 of these were Francophones. Francophone federal employees stationed in Quebec or

alists still use the statistics of the 1940s, 1950s or early 1960s, the same data which got tremendous publicity in the early 1960s when the first "independence" organizations started their campaign.

Similar statistical battles surround the sensitive issue of federal expenditures in Quebec. The final destination of federal expenditures is not determined easily. Some expenditures, such as transfers to individuals or institutions, are easily accounted for: of the total federal expenditures in these areas, between 22 and 28 per cent have gone to Quebec every year since 1961. However, salaries paid to federal employees, government investments, and federal purchases of goods and services can be accounted in two different ways: according to the location of the expenditures, or on a pro rata basis. The first method, used by Quebec, is based on the hypothesis that the only expenditures which benefit Quebec are those which are made in Quebec or to Quebecers (in or out of Quebec). The other method, used by Ottawa, is based on the hypothesis that direct federal expenditures (those which are not transfers) benefit every Canadian on a pro rata basis wherever they are made.

The same difficulties underlie the accounting of tax receipts. Some of the federal taxes collected in a province are really paid by residents of other provinces. Quebec experts consider that the net transfer of the tax burden is impossible to measure and they hypothesize that this net transfer is limited. Ottawa experts argue that excise and tariff revenue, as well as federal sales tax revenue, have to be attributed to the various parts of Canada according to their share of the gross national product.

Altogether, from Quebec's perspective, the federal government, between 1960 and 1970, took an average of 20 to 24 per cent of federal tax receipts in Quebec, but Quebec was the final destination of approximately 19 to 21 per cent of the federal government's expenditures and transfers. The discrepancy accounts for as much as three per cent in the difference between Quebec's per capita income and Canadian per capita income for most years during the period 1960-1970. (See table 3 for Quebec data.)

in the Ottawa region numbered 64,669 (out of 69,191 Francophones federal employees in the whole of Canada).

Improvement in Francophone representation has been important in the area covered by the Public Service Commission, but much less so in the armed forces (120,000 people), and in the 60 corporations and agencies not covered by the Public Service Commission.

Table 4 – Tax Receipts and Expenditures of the Federal Government in Quebec, 1961–1975 (in millions of dollars)

	1961	1964	1967	1970	1973	1974	1975
Total expenditures	1315	1592	2160	3227	4944	6929	8775
Tax receipts	1906	2312	2755	3742	5107	6387	6754
Difference	− 591	− 720	− 595	− 515	− 163	542	2021

Source: *Comptes économique du Québec*, Ministry of Industry and Commerce, Québec, April 1, 1977.

According to Quebec economic accounts, the situation has improved gradually since 1970, and by 1974 Quebec residents received more from the federal treasury than they contributed. To some degree this reversal was engineered by the Trudeau government as a way to combat the Quebec separatist movement: the idea was labelled "le fédéralisme rentable" (profitable federalism) by Quebec Liberals, who won two provincial elections (1970 and 1973) with that slogan.

On the expenditure side, three main mechanisms have been put into effect: new hiring practices consonant with the Official Languages Act, better advertising in Quebec of federal tenders for supply and services, and a general bias in favor of Canada's economically depressed areas in federal programs (a map of these areas can be obtained from the Department of Regional Economic Expansion, established in 1969). On the transfer side, programs such as unemployment insurance, welfare and equalization payments are inherently biased in favor of economically depressed areas: the Trudeau government put more money into existing transfer programs and created new ones specifically directed to the economically depressed areas (for instance Opportunities for Youth, the Local Initiatives Program, and the Regional Economic Expansion program). For the new programs, budgets were generally divided among regions according to their percentage of Canadian unemployed: when Quebec had 40 per cent of Canada's unemployed, 40 per cent of the "expansion" program budget was channeled to Quebec. Moreover, perhaps in order to make sure that the objectives were correctly pursued, the departments most concerned with these programs were often administered by French-Canadian ministers (such as Jean-Pierre Goyer, Jean Marchand, Gérard Pelletier, and Jean Chrétien).

Finally, on the taxation side, the federal government has raised the level of personal exemptions for income tax purposes, introduced various tax postponement schemes (such as the Registered Retirement Savings Plan), included capital gains in the definition of taxable income, and maintained stiff progressive rates in income tax. These and other tax changes have led to a *relative* reduction of the total personal income tax burden in the poorer provinces, including Quebec, as compared with the better-off central and western provinces.

As a consequence of all these policies, as well as of the federal oil-pricing policy and of the stagnation and inflation that have severely hit Quebec and the eastern provinces since 1973, federal payments in Quebec have exceeded federal tax receipts from Quebec in the last few years, even according to Parti Québécois arithmetic. However, members of the Parti Québécois continue to refer to the statistics of the 1960 to 1970 period, dated statistics which had been widely publicized by two popular nationalist leaders, Jacques Parizeau and Claude Morin (the latter in two best sellers: *Le pouvoir québécois... en négociation* and *Le combat québécois*).

Quebecers who work for the Parti Québécois are prone to use statistics which "prove" that the federal government has neglected French Canadians. They are also aware of the relative failure of the bilingualization scheme in terms of French Quebec representation in the federal public service. Those who know that for the last few years, at least, federalism has indeed produced a net transfer to Quebec, such as provincial cabinet ministers Bernard Landry and Rodrigue Tremblay, explain that welfare payments are not what Quebec needs. They show that among federal expenditures in Quebec, transfer payments stand out. In their view, transfer payments, however large, have not compensated for the outflow of capital which afflicted Quebec from 1960 to 1973.[7]

Meeting Parti Québécois workers during the 1973 and 1976 electoral campaigns brought to light a dozen other arguments against the spending policies of the federal government. Some of these arguments have also been mentioned, since their advent to power, by Parti Québécois ministers: the auto pact with the United States, Canadian agriculture policy, Canadian National Railways and Air Canada fares. (See box for contrasting viewpoints expressed by Parti Québécois minister Bernard Landry and Liberal economist André Raynauld.)

Given that the Quebec economy has its problems, who or what is to blame?

Poor productivity, lack of capable managers and the costs of being different from the rest of the country, answers André Raynauld, former chairman of the Economic Council of Canada and currently Liberal MNA for Outremont.

The national policy created by Sir John A. Macdonald and continued by successive federal governments, according to Bernard Landry, provincial minister of economic development and close confidant of Prime Minister Lévesque.

The two men were carrying on the continuing debate on the economics of federalism this morning at a meeting of the Association of Quebec Economists. Although both agreed that the economy of Quebec is backward and underdeveloped, there was little else in the way of common ground.

[As Mr. Raynauld argued], the traditional role of the Church, French-Canadian attitudes to education and business, to risk taking, to work and leisure have all played their part in the evolution of two labor markets—one English and advanced, and the other French and backward.

Source: *The Montreal Star*, April 21, 1977, pages 1 and 2 (a report by Noel Wright).

According to Parti Québécois members, the Trudeau government has been able to do something for Quebec only by taking advantage of the threat felt by English-speaking Canada as a result of the growth of the Quebec nationalist parties. But Trudeau's solutions do not answer the needs of Quebec. According to Parti Québécois ministers, what Quebec needs most is industrial investment in its small communities, which are burdened with excessive dependency rates. In most of these communities, unemployment runs in the 20-to-25-percent range and the labor force accounts for less than half the adult population. In order to develop the economic capabilities of the French-speaking inhabitants of these small Quebec localities, Parti Québécois leaders say that Quebec needs all available public resources and legislative powers—half of which are in the hands of the federal government.

How to Remedy Quebec's Economic Lag?

The causes of the Quebec economic lag are numerous: lack of geographical mobility, lower educational levels, and structural problems related to demography and industry. Quebec has a number of primary industries which follow a fluctuating world market; it has a number of secondary industries which are undergoing a modernization process under severe market difficulties; it has public services which have become inflated out of proportion in response to social and economic problems. Quebec also suffers from absentee ownership of the larger corporations in its leading sectors. All these factors combine to give Quebec a lower per capita income, a higher rate of unemployment, and insufficient industrial investment. French-Canadian nationalists, and notably Parti Québécois ministers, would add that the division of legislative and administrative powers hinders the search for solutions.

French Canadians, experts and laymen, agree on the objectives: the increased well-being and economic capability of French Canadians as a group and of individual French Canadians and the survival of the French language. There is also general agreement on definite remedies. People know that collective productivity has to grow, through mechanization, automation, organization, ideas, market research, education, better use of available manpower. But to achieve this, resources are needed: savings have to be channeled toward productive industrial investment, dysfunctions have to be eliminated and so forth. Members of the Parti Québécois believe that none of this is within reach if a collective will to gain a national economic capability is not instilled in Quebec's population and if governmental institutions are not restructured to give the Quebec government full and unified power over all the levers of collective action in Quebec. Those who oppose the Parti Québécois either do not regard Quebec's economic problems as being as serious as the Parti Québécois does, or believe that they can be solved within the same institutional structures in which the economic difficulties have grown.

It may be that the Quebec government does not have to worry (see box). The educational reforms in Quebec have already started to produce results; Quebec's young people now rank among the best educated in Canada. The birthrate has been reduced below the Canadian average and the demographic structure is improving; the percentage of the population that is of working age will increase to a point significantly above that of other industrialized nations, partly because of a lower life expectancy in Quebec. The opening up of European markets for primary resources will probably lead to a new era of industrialization in Quebec. Social measures already in operation, such as nurseries, adult training, and part-time work facilities, will lead to further increases in productive capabilities. Language can even be seen as an advantage, with Quebec being able to benefit from two sources of innovation, the United States and western Europe.

At the Royal Bank, we have confidence in Quebec. Quebec, indeed, has a vigorous and diversified economy. Its industrial and economic profile is almost identical to that of the rest of Canada: for example, it has pretty much the same proportion of companies in the manufacturing sector, pretty much the same proportion of resource industries, pretty much the same proportion of financial and other service industries, etc. Quebec is far from being an underdeveloped province. The rest of Canada should not think of Quebec as having a simple economy, lacking in capital, specialized manpower, imagination or resources. It's not the case. Quebec has a vigorous economy.

W. Earle McLaughlin, chairman and president of the Royal Bank of Canada, speaking in Montreal, April 18, 1977.

Source: *La Presse*, Montreal, April 20, 1977.

Still, the leaders of Quebec's political parties believe that Quebec's economic problems will not disappear unless there is some government action. But the specific measures advocated vary widely according to the perception each leader has of the causes of Quebec's economic lag. Economists who explain Quebec problems by pointing to the shift to the west, such as Liberal André Raynauld, believe that Quebec must do everything to remain within the attraction zone of this golden west, and they favor the maintenance of Canadian federalism and the industrial renaissance of Montreal. Those who believe in the "linguistic discrimination hypothesis", and in federal neglect of French Canadians, as do Parti Québécois ministers, advocate Quebec political sovereignty. Others, who believe in the "cultural differentiation cost", generally favor compromises between Quebec and Ottawa. But there is a common denominator behind all of these: nearly all opinion leaders favor an improvement in the material well-being of French Canadians.

3

The Idea of a Homeland

Material well-being is not everything. It is far from being all that Quebec French Canadians yearn for. Indeed, Quebec French Canadians who favor an increase in their collective well-being do not want to give up any of their cultural or social particularities as a price for such an increase. One thing is clear: most French Canadians living in Quebec and in the bordering regions want, at the same time, to keep using French *and* to increase their collective well-being. Material well-being is the dominant objective for many; national survival is the dominant objective for others; but most French Canadians agree on the crucial importance of both these objectives.

Moreover, a great many of them want to reach a third objective which has little to do with material well-being, but has extreme emotional value. They would like the territory they inhabit to be their homeland, a territory where they can live with total dignity, permanently free from the frustration now imposed on them by what they see as economic inequalities drawn along language lines, free from the frustration now imposed on them by a political system dominated by "others". By and large, Quebec's French Canadians are ready to support changes which would let them feel more at home in Quebec.

Unlike the other two collective objectives pursued by a large proportion of the French-speaking population of Quebec and neighboring regions, the idea of a national homeland challenges the present Canadian constitutional framework. The language problem could be largely solved by a measure of territorial unilingualism, or by improvements in the bilingual solution that has been tried since 1968. Settling the economic problem does not necessarily require a constitutional reorganization. But the idea of a national homeland necessarily challenges the current Canadian constitutional framework. In this sense, Pierre Trudeau, Prime Minister of Canada, was perfectly aware of the realities of the situation when he said, after the Quebec election of November 15, 1976, that the real question was, "Can francophones of Quebec consider Canada as their country, or must they feel at home only in Quebec?"

Surprisingly, the idea of a national homeland for French-speaking Quebecers does not seem to worry the English-speaking experts who comment on Quebec. The language problems and the economic problems seem more pressing, and they make the headlines and are described in detail. But nationalist feelings, which are really the root of the matter, are neglected altogether. People will say: "What Quebec really wants is more control over all things cultural; what Quebec wants is a series of specific concessions; what Quebec really wants is this, or that." No one mentions the fundamental desire: a homeland for a nation. In my view, as a conclusion drawn from years of reading and interviewing, it is on this idea of a "true" homeland for French-speaking Quebecers that Parti Québécois leaders will try to unite Quebec. The other objectives, language and economics, coincide with this third objective, but this one alone necessarily leads to the demand for sovereignty.

Territorial Symbols

Those who hold the view that French Canadians can feel at home only in Quebec have succeeded in changing the label by which Quebec French Canadians identify themselves. Fifteen years ago, nobody in Quebec would have used the term "Québécois" to designate an inhabitant of the Province of Quebec: this label was applied only to the inhabitants of Quebec City. The French-speaking inhabitants of the province of Quebec were called French Canadians, just like "Francophones" in the other provinces of Canada. Only the French-speaking inhabitants of the maritime provinces, who were descendants of the French settlers who came to "Acadia" (now New Brunswick and Nova Scotia) in the seventeenth and early eighteenth centuries, had a separate name: Acadians. In the St. Lawrence Valley, the French settlers of the same period had taken the name of "Canadiens", because their territory, New France, was locally known as Canada. Indeed, for more than 150 years after the British conquest of New France in 1759-1760, the French-speaking inhabitants of Canada described themselves as "les Canadiens" and labelled the English-speaking newcomers "les Anglais". After Confederation, the expression

"French Canadian" progressively displaced the former appellation. And now, in the 1970s, a large proportion of French-speaking Quebecers call themselves "les Québécois" (and they include under this term any inhabitant of the province of Quebec who considers Quebec his homeland).

During the 1960s, several surveys included questions about the ethnic loyalties of French-speaking Canadians, but normally these surveys made no reference to the term "Québécois", because that term was not yet in general use in Quebec. In these surveys of the 1960s, respondents were asked whether they considered themselves French Canadians or simply Canadians. These surveys showed that 20 to 25 per cent identified themselves as "French Canadians only", and 40 to 60 per cent as "French Canadians first", with the remainder (between 20 and 35 per cent, depending on the survey) saying they were "Canadians first". The first known survey of the whole Quebec population to use the word "Québécois" was conducted in 1970, a few years after the new name had begun to become popular. This survey, conducted by sociologist Maurice Pinard, revealed that, of a sample of 4,889 French-speaking Quebec adults, 21 per cent considered themselves "Québécois", 44 per cent "French Canadians", 34 per cent "Canadians", and one per cent something else. According to Parti Québécois sources, private surveys completed between 1973 and 1976 indicate that a majority of French-speaking Quebecers now call themselves "Québécois".

This increasing popularity of the term "Québécois" shows how important the territorial symbol of Quebec is in the social thinking of contemporary French-speaking Quebecers. In a way, those who label themselves "Québécois" express their political loyalty to the society bounded by Quebec frontiers, Quebec values and Quebec institutions. But a political loyalty is rarely exclusive. People who express a loyalty to their country generally feel related to both larger and smaller territorial symbols as well: North America, the Western World, a province, a region, a city. However, one of these loyalties is generally dominant. A "true" Canadian is a Canadian first, then a Manitoban, Albertan or whatever. In Quebec, currently, fewer than one third of French-speaking adults consider themselves "Canadians first". When asked which government they favor, Ottawa or Quebec, four French-speaking Quebecers out of ten say Quebec, one says Ottawa, two say both, two say neither, and one starts to argue. Outside Quebec, six English-speaking Canadians out of ten favor Ottawa, and only one

favors his provincial government (two others say both, and one neither), or roughly so.[8] According to the survey data used on the CBC
radio program *Sunday Morning* on April 3, 1977, when asked which
government they think of when asked "which government is yours",
50.7 per cent of the Quebec respondents of both languages said
Quebec and 32.7 per cent said Ottawa.

ENOUGH, MR. LEVESQUE!

**You are about to pass legislation which will
be seen as regressive and discriminatory. And
we know why. You're trying to scare us out. Why
else would anyone propose a language policy
like yours?**

**Well, Mr. Levesque, your tactic almost
worked. But consider this: We have stopped
running.**

**We are staying in Canada. What's more, as
long as this remains a democratic society, we
demand that our rights, including all rights of
language use, be protected. We demand it for
ourselves, our children and for the conduct of
business.**

**Pursue your dream, Mr. Levesque, and we will
pursue ours — a Quebec based on respect for
human rights. West Quebec, Canada.
The eleventh province.**

*Note to all Quebecers:
We need your time and
your money, your hands
and your hearts.
Please direct your
enquiries, and send
your contributions to:*

THE PREPARATORY
COMMITTEE FOR
AN 11th PROVINCE

P.O. Box 998,
Station H, Montreal,
H3G 2M9.

Source: *The Montreal Star*, April 30, 1977, page A-13.

In Quebec, contrary to the norm in the rest of Canada, the dominant loyalty of the largest number is addressed to the symbols of the province, and not to those of Canada. This loyalty, however, is restrained by conflicting views related to other rallying symbols. Thus, according to a small survey conducted in 1968 by political scientist H. D. Forbes among Quebec youth, 77 per cent of the 699 young people who answered the question said that they considered the whole of Canada as their country and only 20 per cent said that their country was restricted to Quebec alone. The survey also showed that individuals were ready to accept several designations in order to identify themselves: 80 per cent of this sample of Quebec youth accepted the term "Québécois" as fitting them (a percentage which far exceeds anything that has been obtained for a sample of the whole population). But, at the same time, 78 per cent of the these respondents accepted the term "Canadien français"; 65 per cent accepted the term "Canadien"; 30 per cent the expression "Américain du Nord", and 15 per cent the word "Français". The loyalty to Quebec exists, but it is (or was) a loyalty tempered by other loyalties. It is clear that many Quebecers see Quebec as their homeland, just as many Canadians see Canada as their homeland. But the idea of Canada, as a territorial symbol, conflicts with the idea many Quebecers have of their homeland. The territory of Canada includes Quebec.

If a break-up of the Canadian federation were to occur, the territorial symbols would undoubtedly lead to fierce arguing about boundaries, because many Quebecers, notably the leading publicists of the independence movement, consider that their part of Canadian territory should be roughly proportional to the percentage traditionally constituted by Quebec in the Canadian population, that is 30 per cent.[9] At present, Quebec territory covers 523,860 square miles, or 15.4 per cent of Canada's 3,560,238 square miles of land. The part of the Quebec continental peninsula known as Labrador, which is now Newfoundland territory, covers 101,881 square miles (3.0 per cent of the total (Canadian surface). The islands located east of the 79° 30′ longitude, north of the Quebec peninsula, account for another 4.6 per cent of Canada. Parti Québécois members who talk about Quebec territory usually consider that in the event of a break-up of Canada, a sovereign Quebec should cover the territory of the province, plus the federal territory east of the 79° 30′ longitude, and the islands in the St. Lawrence, plus possibly Labrador. Labrador was awarded to the then Dominion of Newfoundland in 1927 by the British Privy Council, in settlement of claims made at the time by Newfoundland and the then separate Dominion of Canada (Newfoundland joined the Canadian federation in 1949). Quebec was the part of Canada which was "truncated" as a consequence of the British Privy Council decision, and the population of Quebec, by and large, has maintained the view that Labrador is "rightly" part of Quebec. In any case, if the Canadian federation were to break up, the territorial vision of Quebec which prevails among "les Québécois" would lead to a lot of aggressive arguing. If the Parti Québécois gains the support of a majority of the Quebec electorate (which constitutes 28 per cent of the Canadian population) in favor of a sovereign state, it will probably insist on at least 20 to 22 per cent of Canadian territory for that state.

It is clear that territorial symbols play a large part in the definition of a "homeland". They even play a part in the expression of loyalties in the daily behavior of many citizens of Canada. Hence the standing joke in Canada of telling people who go into or out of Quebec not to forget their passports. When a Quebecer says he is "a Canadian first", there can be no doubt that he considers the whole territory of Canada *his* country. This is a psychological response, for he has been told that this part of the world belongs to Canadians, that a Canadian is at home everywhere within the borders of this vast area. He loves the picture of beautiful Lake Louise in the Canadian Rockies, or of charming Nova Scotian coves, and even if he has never been out of Quebec, he cherishes such scenes as his private property—just as English-speaking Canadians hold to the landscape of the Gaspé coast or picturesque Quebec City. Territorial symbols carry deep significance for many people. The idea that a territory can be a "property" dominates the whole world: indeed the whole world has been divided into pieces, and it is a life objective for millions of individuals to acquire a small piece of land that would be "private property". Naturally, territorial symbols, and eagerness to own land, lead to conflicts over the most desirable resource on earth: a place in the sun.

Quebecers who want to bring about Quebec's accession to sovereignty thus want to establish their "shared property claims" over the territory which they consider the homeland of the Québécois. These Quebecers do not identify themselves with English-speaking Canadians living outside Quebec, but they feel themselves to be members of a "new and developing" Quebec society. They consider Lake Louise and Peggy's Cove foreign beauty spots, just as Switzerland, Rome or Washington, D.C. are nice places to be in, but places which do not "belong" to Quebecers: what belongs to Quebecers is Quebec.

Area and Power

Property rights over a piece of land imply a definite control by the owner over his territory. The whole idea of private ownership of land is to endow individuals with unquestioned authority over an area: the principle of private ownership, on which most people agree, enables individuals to "reign" supreme over an area of known dimensions, without having to resort to force or violence in order to establish their sovereignty.

Many Quebecers feel that they are "outsiders" when they go out of Quebec to other Canadian provinces. At the same time, they feel that "outsiders" (that is, Canadians from other provinces) have a lot of say about what goes on in Quebec. Many Quebecers, moreover, have the feeling that they have no say in Canadian affairs, and can influence no government other than that of Quebec.[10] According to a survey conducted in 1968 by political scientist John Meisel, 58 per cent of the 632 French-speaking respondents of the Quebec sample felt that they had no say in Canadian politics; only 34 per cent of the 927 Ontario respondents had such a feeling. Statistics on the relative interest shown in federal and provincial elections illustrate similar attitudes. Voter turnout in the last few Quebec provincial elections has hovered between 80 and 85 per cent, while it stands in the 60-to-75-percent range in provincial elections held in other parts of Canada. Conversely, while voting turnout in federal elections reaches 80 per cent in English-speaking Canada, it stays around 70 per cent in French-speaking Quebec. For many Quebec voters, the government of Quebec is theirs, while the federal government of Canada is the government of English-speaking Canadians.

Quebecers who feel that way naturally wish for more powers over their own area for the government which they consider their own. Such attitudes reflect the sense of belonging to that particular society defined by the French language, the territorial symbols of Quebec, and Quebec-based institutions. However these attitudes are not held with the same degree of intensity by all Quebecers: loyalties are divided, and a majority of Quebec voters are confused or ambiguous on the question of identifying *their* government, *their* territory, and *their* reference group.

In spite of this ambiguity, when asked to express their position on the debate between the Parti Québécois and the federal government, a majority of French-speaking Quebecers say they favor the concession of more powers to the Quebec government. In a 1973 survey conducted by a McGill University research team led by Richard Hamilton and Maurice Pinard, among 861 French-speaking respondents 13 per cent said they were in favor of Quebec independence, and another 39 per cent said they wished that more powers would be transferred from Ottawa to Quebec; only three per cent of this sample wished that Quebec could transfer powers to Ottawa, while 21 per cent were in favor of maintaining the existing division of powers between the two governments (23 per cent had no opinion). The CBC *Sunday Morning* survey (April 3, 1977) revealed that 35.5 per cent of the people interviewed in a representative sample of French and English Quebecers were in favor of maintaining the existing division of powers. On the other hand 38.6 per cent favored an extension of Quebec's powers, 12.4 per cent favored an extension of Ottawa's powers, and 13.5 per cent abstained.

It is safe to hypothesize that the fundamental motivation behind Quebecers' opinions in favor of Quebec independence or increased autonomy is related to the sense of identity felt in relation to the French-speaking society of Quebec. Indeed, another survey conducted by Maurice Pinard in 1970 revealed that, among 795 respondents who said that they favored Quebec's secession from Canada, 52 per cent said that they were motivated by "nationalistic" economic reasons; these economic reasons were of the following type: "*We* would become stronger; *our* savings would stay home; *we* would administer *our* resources *ourselves*; *our* taxes would be reduced...." The other respondents favoring Quebec secession did not mention a motivation related to economics, but were motivated by sentiments such as cultural independence, improved collective status, reduction of ethnic tensions and so on.

Conversely, the fear of possible Quebec secession depends little on nationalist attitudes but rather almost entirely on economic insecurity. Both before and after independence, a secessionist country usually finds some of its outside markets cut off for various reasons. During the transition period leading to secession, clashes between extremist groups for and against separation cause chaos and violence and lead to economic stagnation. In the case of Quebec, leading entrepreneurs and managers could exile themselves and leave Quebec without economic leadership, the prey of leftists. Economic fears are held by the leading opponents of the Parti Québécois, and the fight against independence is essentially based on the fear of economic losses.[11]

Surprisingly, however, few people ever argue for or against Quebec independence from an institutional viewpoint. Institutional arguments and references to particular aspects of the federal set-up or to questions related to federal-provincial relations rarely show up in the answers obtained to open questions about Quebec independence asked by sociologists or political scientists who conduct surveys in Quebec or Canada as a whole.

Quebec and Canadian Federalism

The average Canadian does not seem to understand that the immediate issue involved in Quebec independence is the federal government's own presence in Quebec. The average Canadian does not even know the correct answers to questions related to the division of powers between the federal and the provincial governments. A Canada-wide survey conducted in 1968 by the Institute for Behavioural Research of Toronto revealed, for instance, that 52 per cent of the respondents did not know that unemployment insurance was a federal responsibility, 38 per cent did not know that foreign affairs were a federal responsibility, and 40 per cent were not aware of the fact that education was a provincial responsibility. Governmental institutions and division of powers are matters which, in the view of a majority of Canadians, do not warrant much attention and do not need to be known with any degree of precision. Indeed, a survey conducted for the Montreal French daily *La Presse* after the 1974 federal election showed that a majority of the voters in the Montreal area went to the polling booths without knowing the name of any local candidate except the Liberal, and with a very scant idea of the problems which had been discussed during the campaign.[12]

The general ignorance of the workings of governmental institutions probably explains the fact that, for a majority of the people, Quebec independence is not naturally related to what it is meant to achieve: a reorganization of governmental institutions operating in Quebec. What the Parti Québécois is for is a peaceful reorganization of the federal system, in terms of the federal presence in Quebec and federal power over Quebec. What is at stake is the federal presence in Quebec.

Although this does not show up in surveys, the federal government is the institution most immediately and directly concerned by the secessionist option of many Quebecers. Indeed, if a break-up of the Canadian federation were to occur, its most perceptible effect would be a reorganization of federal departments, offices and crown corporations. It has been estimated that between 15 and 20 per cent of federal employees would stop working under the authority of the federal government and start working under the authority of the Quebec government. Most of the federal employees likely to be involved are already residents of Quebec and work in offices located either in Quebec or in the federal capital. It has been estimated that about two thirds of the personnel involved would not even need to move to another office building; among the rest, however, there are several thousand who would have to move from Ottawa to Montreal or Quebec City. The moving of several thousand households subsequent to a governmental reorganization is the *minimum* to be expected as a consequence of Quebec's accession to sovereignty.

This governmental reorganization, in the view of Parti Québécois leaders, is the only means available to French-speaking Quebecers who want to apply in Quebec policies which differ from those which are applied in the rest of Canada. On many questions which are now the responsibility of the federal government, French-speaking Quebecers hold views which differ from those of English-speaking Canadians: this is the case in matters of language, culture, scientific development, communications, agriculture, trade, and so on. French Canadians are poorly represented in the associations which lobby in Ottawa, and they are a minority in every federal committee or council. When the demands from Quebec differ from those of Ontario, the latter are likely to prevail, and the French-Canadian representatives cannot easily obtain "special treatment" for Quebec.

With a declining proportion of the total Canadian population, French-speaking Quebecers (now between 20 and 23 per cent of Canada) cannot hope to dominate the government side of the Canadian House of Commons any more.* However, French-speaking members of Parliament have constituted between 40 and 55 per cent of the government benches since 1896, except for the periods of Conservative rule: 1911-1921, 1930-1935 and 1957-1963, or 21 of the last 81 years.

---

* The 1971 census found 3,668,000 inhabitants of Quebec who stated that they spoke French only; 713,000 others had French as their mother tongue but were able to speak both French and English; and 522,000 more, who spoke both French and English, did not have French as their mother tongue. Out of 21,568,000 inhabitants of Canada (1971), unilingual French-speaking Quebecers account for 17 per cent of the population of the country. Quebecers who speak French, whatever their mother tongue, account for 23 per cent of the total Canadian population.

Such a feat was achieved because Quebec sent a solid bloc of Liberal representatives to the House of Commons, while English-speaking Canadians were more or less evenly divided between Liberals and Conservatives. In federal elections, Quebec helped the Liberal party and kept it in power. But, even with its overrepresentation on the government side of Parliament, Quebec never obtained more than one third of the Cabinet posts, and the Quebec ministers in Ottawa were not able to introduce even such timid measures as French words on the federal cheques issued to Quebec residents until the 1960s, when bombs began to explode in Quebec and showed how exasperated some Quebecers had become.

In spite of the leadership of Prime Minister Trudeau after 1968, a number of Quebec interests have been frustrated by federal policies. The priority of the Trudeau Cabinet has been "Canadian unity" and measures which would have upheld Quebec's autonomist positions have generally been brushed aside. The Quebec government position on a constitutional amendment formula for Canada has been perhaps the most significant case; another case has been the Quebec government position on social affairs; a third one, the Quebec government position concerning communications. Among less publicized questions which have raised problems in the area of "national unity", one can mention the negotiations on the James Bay hydro project, the debate on container terminals, production quotas and subsidies in agriculture, tariff negotiations, immigration, Quebec's international relations, the Quebec Pension Plan, Quebec housing policies, and many others.

When the Quebec government states a position which runs against the federal position, it usually does so for reasons related to Quebec's particular circumstances: its demographic structure, its industrial structure, its foreign markets and types of exports, its language, and other distinctive characteristics.

Although they could not detail what powers should be held by Quebec, a majority of French-speaking Quebecers are aware of the situation in which French-speaking Quebecers find themselves when dealing with the federal government. A large part of the news related to the Canadian government in the Quebec media consists of conflicting statements uttered by Quebec and Ottawa ministers on some aspect or other of their continuing quarrel. And it is not surprising that a majority of French-speaking Quebecers consider the division of powers a source of waste which could be eliminated by giving one single government complete authority over the areas where conflicting interests lead Ottawa and Quebec to confront each other.

Quebec's Case Against the Federal Government

The Quebec provincial government has been the upholder of the interests of French Canadians since 1867. And in the view of Quebec nationalists these interests have regularly been at odds with those of the rest of the Canadian population. The federal government has, for instance, undertaken the building of railways and canals which have served the interests of the English-speaking population of the country and of Montreal, but it has neglected the areas of Quebec inhabited by French Canadians. The federal government, between 1914 and 1918 and between 1939 and 1945, greatly developed the industrial capacity of Canada, but did so to the benefit primarily of southern Ontario and, to a lesser extent, of English-speaking Montreal. By and large, the federal government of Canada, since 1867, has been the government of English-speaking Canadians and the government of Quebec has been the government of French Canadians.

The Quebec case against the federal government is not a case against federalism; it is a case against a system prejudicial to French Canadians. Federalism is based on the idea that the areas of governmental action where conflicts are likely to develop along territorial lines should fall under the authority of territorial governments, while the areas of governmental action where various territories can find a common interest should be administered by a common, central, federal government. The Canadian federation developed a division of powers between the provincial governments, on one side, and the central government, on the other side, which was an application of the federal principle to the particular circumstances of the British North American colonies in 1867. Matters of local interest, which could not fit into any single Canadian standard, were left to the provinces. These provincial concerns included education, a particularly delicate question in a country where two language groups and various religious denominations coexisted. Provincial powers also included the administration of natural resources and agriculture (the latter falling also under federal jurisdiction in its more general aspects). In addition, the provincial jurisdiction covered local government as well as public services and regulations established for local purposes or private objectives.

The authority of the provincial governments was delineated in a restrictive manner in four sections of the constitutional statute which created the Dominion of Canada in 1867 (sections 92, 93, 94 and 95 of the British North America Act, 1867). The authority of the central government, on the other hand, was stated in very broad terms in one section of the statute (section 91) and reiterated in the sections relating to the provinces so as to restrict the extension of provincial powers. Paragraph 10 of section 92 stated that the Canadian Parliament had control over interprovincial communications and over public works which it considered of general Canadian interest. Section 93 gave the Canadian government the authority to interfere in educational matters if the rights of denominational schools established before 1867 were being threatened by provincial legislation. Section 95 stated that both the federal Parliament and the provincial legislatures could make laws relating to agriculture and immigration but that the federal laws would have precedence.

In its division of legislative powers, the British North America Act of 1867 put the central government in a dominant position. The new Canadian government had authority over practically every area of governmental action except those which related to municipalities, education and local matters. In the area of tax revenue, the central government found itself with 60 per cent of all taxation receipts in Canada, the provinces and municipalities being left with the greatly unpopular direct taxation (which, in any case, the central government could also use). Moreover, the federal government was given the power to disallow provincial legislation which ran counter to federal interests (this federal power over provincial legislation was described in sections 55, 56, 57 and 90 of the Act).

Administrative powers in the provinces were to be held by a federal nominee, the Lieutenant-Governor (sections 58 and 59 of the Act). In 1878 and again in 1891, the Lieutenant-Governor of Quebec used his authority and tried to curb provincial initiatives, in spite of constitutional practice which had already restricted the powers of the Lieutenant-Governor in other provinces. This federal control over Quebec, through the Lieutenant-Governor, led to two serious crises, one in 1878, the other in 1891-1892. Canadian Senators are also nominated by the federal government and they are in no way representatives of "provincial interests".

In the view of the Fathers of Confederation, the areas of governmental action which were left to the provincial governments were indeed very limited. But the history of the Canadian federation has proved that the Fathers of Confederation underestimated the conflicts which could arise in the areas of responsibility awarded to the federal government. Federal policies in several areas benefited some provinces at the expense of others, and as early as 1870 provincial governments began to fight to protect aggrieved regional interests. Nova Scotia felt so underprivileged during the first 30 years of Confederation that its provincial government came to take serious autonomist stands. So did Quebec, especially after 1886. Later, it would be Alberta and British Columbia. The pressure put on the federal government to let the provincial governments take initiatives gradually led to a reassessment of the division of powers in the Canadian federation. New areas of government action were opened and left to the provinces (roads for automobiles, electricity, natural resource development, etc.), while others were taken by the central government (radio, foreign affairs, unemployment insurance, family allowances, pensions, etc.).

While Canadian federalism was evolving according to the circumstances, reflecting the interplay of political forces and regional interests, Quebec became more and more dissatisfied and its government took autonomist positions more and more frequently. It introduced new taxes in 1882 (corporation taxes) and in 1892 (succession duties), and was among the first to resort to corporate income taxes (1932), personal income taxes (1939) and sales taxes (1940). It showed its opposition to federal involvement in such matters as prohibition (notably on the occasion of a 1898 plebiscite on the subject), agriculture (notably between 1911 and 1920), welfare payments, including pensions and unemployment insurance (notably during the 1930s).[13] Quebec rejected federal proposals related to taxation from 1945 to 1957 and obtained the establishment of a federal program of equalization payments. In the 1960s, an opting-out formula to be applied to federal grants to provincial governments was established at Quebec's insistence, and the Quebec government was the only one to take advantage of the formula: instead of benefiting from federal grants, Quebec gained access to tax rebates.

For more than 40 years now the Quebec government has generally provided the main institutional opposition to governmental centralization or policy standardization in Canada. It was often the only government to oppose federal initiatives. It is the only provincial government that maintains services in many areas in which the federal government has the monopoly of action outside Quebec. In Quebec, there is a full-fledged Department of Revenue, which reaches into the pocket of every individual and corporate taxpayer in Quebec. No other province has such an organization. The Quebec government has a disguised department of foreign affairs, with delegations in a dozen foreign cities, intergovernmental agreements in several areas, regular exchange programs, and so on. No other province in Canada has anything approaching this, not even Ontario. The Quebec government has a Department of Immigration, as does Ontario: Quebec has a Department of Communications, with a provincial radio and television corporation (Radio-Quebec). In the field of agriculture, Quebec maintains the most extensive provincial services in Canada. In the field of labor, Quebec maintains manpower centres, the only provincial manpower centres in Canada. Quebec also maintains a provincial police, a provincial pension plan, a provincial housing corporation, a provincial film board, and dozens of other provincial offices, commissions and services which one rarely finds in other provinces.

There are very few areas of governmental activity in which the Quebec government has not established its own services which compete, on Quebec territory, with federal services in the same areas. This competition is visible not only to Quebec civil servants but to thousands of Quebecers and is resented as sheer insanity, not only because it wastes millions of dollars but also because the provincial programs are generally considered better suited to Quebec needs, while lacking the budgets necessary in order to be effective.

Parti Québécois activists object to the federal government's moves toward centralization, because they believe that decisions taken in Ottawa are taken either by English-speaking senior bureaucrats or by committees where English-speaking civil servants or ministers are a majority. In the view of Quebec nationalists, Ottawa decisions made by French Canadians are extremely rare, and decisions which favor Quebec or Quebec interests generally reflect the impact of crises such as the Quebec terrorism of the 1960s or the growth of Parti Québécois support in the 1970s. When a decision is taken in Ottawa, it is generally the result of pressures put on the decision-makers by interest groups in which French Canadians are a silent minority. English-speaking civil servants are linked to all kinds of interests and they usually try to defend those interests, just as French-speaking civil servants do—but, at the decision-making levels, for every French-speaking civil servant one finds four or five English-speaking civil servants. When Ottawa launches a new program, such as the 1971 Opportunities for Youth project or the 1972 Local Initiatives Program, applications for jobs, subsidies and information coming from English-speaking Canadians flow in for several weeks before such applications start to come in from French-speaking Quebecers in any number. This is probably explained by the "grapevine effect": more English-speaking applicants hear about the program first.

Among examples of federal decisions considered detrimental to French Canadians, those which come up most often are immigration, certain welfare programs, federal actions in the cultural sector, and the auto pact. But other examples abound: the Borden line for oil imports, freight rates, and so on. Nationalists like to quote immigration statistics*: between 1901 and 1964, out of 8,089,823 immigrants to Canada, only 112,740 were French, that is 1.5 per cent of the total. Among the immigrants of other than British or French origin who opted to live in Quebec, three out of four chose English as their "official" language.**

When European governments started their welfare programs in the 1920s, pressure mounted in Toronto and other large cities of Canada for old-age pensions and similar transfer payments. At the time, older citizens accounted for eight per cent of Ontario's population but they accounted for less than four per cent of Quebec's French-speaking population. By having Ottawa pay for old-age pensions, the English-speaking pressure groups angered Quebec civil servants who saw no need for such pensions in Quebec and considered that their province had more pressing needs than old-age pensions, even though they were seen as a generous idea. The federal law was enacted in 1927, and Quebec, in 1936, was the last province to sign the agreement.

In the 1950s, English-speaking Canadians became aware of the cultural impact on Canada of the United States, and pressure groups started a campaign for federal action on the cultural sector. French-speaking Quebecers, at the time, felt no threat from the United States culture industry; on the contrary, they were of the opinion that "cul-

---

* See Rosaire Morin, *L'immigration au Canada* (Montreal: Les Editions de l'Action nationale, 1966). Morin quotes Pierre Laporte (page 144) who, as a minister of the Quebec government, declared on February 10, 1965, "It is clear that immigration as organized by the government of Canada has not been organized in the cultural interests of French Canada." (*Journal des Débats*, 1965, p. 464, translation).

** In 1961, according to census data, in the Montreal metropolitan area, 97 per cent of the 1,353,480 people of French origin had French as their mother tongue; 5.6 per cent of the 377,625 people of British origin had French as their mother tongue (93.92 per cent had English) and 23.72 per cent of the 135,731 people of other origins had chosen French as their "official" language, while 76.32 per cent had chosen English.

ture" was the main reason for the existence of a provincial government and were in favor of provincial action in this sector. Quebec fought against the federal decision to finance cultural programs. Quebec lost. Millions of dollars were spent by the federal government in various programs which primarily benefited English-speaking individuals and their institutions. Between 1960 and 1975, according to available statistics, French-speaking Quebecers and their institutions got less than 15 per cent of the hundreds of millions of dollars which were spent in federal scientific and cultural grants, subsidies and research contracts.

In the 1960s, Ontario and the federal government became concerned about the huge deficits registered in the Canadian trade in automobiles, trucks and auto parts. An agreement was negotiated with the United States and with the leading American car-makers. The Quebec government at the same time was trying to attract European and Japanese car-makers in order to start a small-car industry in Quebec. Quebec's interests were at odds with those of Ontario. According to Quebec spokesmen, the European car-makers received no help from the federal government. The Canada-United States auto pact led to a substantial increase in industrial activity in Ontario, which had an inflationary effect that was not compensated for by counter-measures in regions suffering from economic stagnation. Quebec was unable to develop an auto industry of any size and it suffered from Ontario-induced inflation; Quebec's economic structure came out of the adventure still more underprivileged.

Immigration policies, welfare programs, cultural and scientific development programs, and the Canada-United States auto pact are only four of a dozen examples Quebec nationalist leaders cite to show how the federal government protects interests which run counter to those of French-speaking Quebecers.* Even though many federal decisions taken since the mid-1960s have had a pro-Quebec bias, the history of Canadian federalism confirms the general feeling held by a majority of French-speaking Quebecers that they would be better served if the Quebec government had a larger share of tax revenues and a monopoly over the numerous areas of government action where French-speaking Quebecers have interests which conflict with those of English-speaking Canadians.

* A periodical such as *L'Action nationale* provides a good survey of these examples.

Theoretical Advantages of Federalism

The belief that the federal government serves the interests of English-speaking Canadians and has a detrimental effect on French-speaking Quebecers has a great impact in Quebec. Moreover, many French-speaking Quebecers fail to see the relevance for the Quebec population of the theoretical advantages of federalism.

The most important theoretical advantage of federalism is the equilibrium that it maintains between two different sets of political institutions, federal and provincial. The institutional balance created by federalism limits the tendency of governments to centralize, to control and to standardize everything. The persistence of regional or provincial governments is a guarantee of some limits to standardization and a minimum degree of territorial dispersion of public expenditures. In a federation, the central government has to face contending power structures which impede its dominating tendencies. In a federation, citizens can turn to another government when they fight against a bureaucracy. In a federation, decisions which serve the interests of the whole country are easily made and obeyed because there is one central authority empowered to reach them; at the same time, territorial governments can safeguard local interests and regional particularisms. This great theoretical advantage of federalism is often quoted by those who take issue with the Parti Québécois.[14] However most nationalists have a fundamental objection to the argument. They approve of the idea of an institutional balance in a federation, but in their view there can be no effective balance if the regional communities are different in size and in culture.

Nevertheless, the idea of making several cultural communities coexist within a large territory and under one set of economic regulations is seen as another great advantage of federalism. Federalism enables different cultural communities to benefit from a common market and from economic structures which permit a better use of productive resources and lead to higher standards of living. Industries which could not develop in any of the individual communities if they were not federated can become profitable and prosper. Such economic benefits can sustain each of the cultural communities and its particular culture. Those who uphold the federal principle in Quebec usually say that Canada, Yugoslavia, Switzerland and India are good examples of coexistence between different and sometimes antagonistic linguistic communities.[15] These four federations, and other federations which have similar features, show the world an example.

From this viewpoint, Canadian federalism can be seen as a great success. Canadians rank among the wealthiest peoples on earth, and the French-speaking minority has succeeded in maintaining its culture and its identity, while benefiting from the general economic prosperity of Canada. The French- and English-speaking communities of Canada have worked together through the federal institutions in relative peace for more than a hundred years. The presence of a French community in Quebec has offered other Canadians the opportunity to know, close to them, a different, great, worldwide culture. However, French-speaking Quebecers who feel threatened by the attractive power of English-speaking North America, notably the leaders of the Parti Québécois, generally believe that the cultural safeguards offered by Canadian federalism are insufficient. They would feel more secure if they could control all the governmental institutions which operate in their territory, while maintaining the economic co-operation that exists among the various regions of Canada.

In some sense, while they may be badly informed on the workings of federal institutions, French-speaking Quebecers often seem very pragmatic when they talk about federalism. They are not impressed by its theoretical advantages. They want to protect the cultural identity of their society and assure it a secure and promising future. They wish that English-speaking Canadians could understand this objective of leaving the Quebec government free to expand its services so as to better safeguard the interests of French-speaking Quebecers (the interests of English-speaking Quebecers being considered as already safeguarded by Quebec's location in North America).

Many politically active French-speaking Quebecers, including Liberals, Conservatives and Péquistes, take great pains to explain that Quebec's French-speaking majority is not anti-English; this majority is only concerned with the survival of the French-speaking "nation" and the economic prosperity of Quebec. These Quebecers believe that nobody but themselves can realize these goals and, as a consequence, only the government controlled by French-speaking Canadians should exert power in Quebec.* But they are aware of the economic con-

---

* The Parti Québécois ministers, now, and the Union Nationale premier, Daniel Johnson, in 1966, have been the best-known exponents of such views.

straints on the ideal of maximum political autonomy for Quebec. In a word, these Quebecers want Quebec to have the greatest amount of political autonomy consistent with the maintenance of beneficial economic relations with the rest of Canada.

Federalism is infinitely varied in its practice. If the European Economic Community is federalism, the "sovereignty-association" scheme put forward by Parti Québécois leaders is also federalism. Federalism in the Canada of the 1970s is very different from the federalism of the 1870s. Canadian federalism differs from West German federalism, which in turn differs from Australian federalism, and so on. Federalism is evolving and adaptable. The flexibility of federalism offers Canadian political leaders the possibility of compromises between English Canada and French Quebec which could satisfy a majority of those who hold to a territorial perception of what their country should be, and who have only a rudimentary knowledge of governmental institutions.

What Quebec Wants

Those French-speaking Quebecers who say that they are "Québécois" and that their homeland is Quebec usually call for a maximization of the Quebec government's power over Quebec territory. These pro-Quebec French Canadians are clearly a majority in Quebec. A majority of French-speaking Quebecers has already supported the Parti Québécois in the November 1976 provincial election. Surveys have shown that between 60 and 75 per cent of French-speaking Quebecers favor an extension of the Quebec government's powers. Approximately 70 per cent of them identify themselves as "Québécois" or as "French Canadians first". The strength of this pro-Quebec feeling, although relatively recent, has been steadily growing for the last two decades.

Surveys of the 1950s and early 1960s conducted by the Canadian Institute of Public Opinion and by Montreal's Groupe de Recherche Sociale showed that, at that time, concern for Quebec provincial autonomy was highly correlated with educational levels. In other words, only the elite was aware of the possibilities of government action in cultural matters. By the mid-1960s, this elite concern with government action and provincial autonomy had gained ground in the French-speaking urban population. In the 1970s, as we have seen, surveys revealed that the trend was being maintained: concern for the future of the French language and the French-speaking population of

Quebec seems to be shared by quite a large proportion of Quebec's population. If this interpretation of available survey data corresponds to reality, there are reasons to believe that nationalist feelings could eventually overcome the economic fears which stand in the way of the Parti Québécois quest for Quebec political independence.

Recent survey data show that a majority of French-speaking Quebecers now agree on a series of fundamental objectives, the first of which relates to the status of the French language in Quebec. According to a study by l'Institut Québécois d'Opinion Publique, published in three Quebec dailies on May 24, 1974, 67 per cent of the French-speaking people surveyed were in favor of making French the only official language of Quebec (19 per cent) or, at least, the priority language (48 per cent). According to the same report, 59 per cent of the French-speaking Quebecers interviewed favored a law making it compulsory for immigrants and immigrants' children to enrol in the French school system. Most English-speaking Quebecers (between 65 and 80 per cent of those who were interviewed, percentages varying according to ethnic origin) favored official bilingualism in Quebec and English schools for Quebec immigrants. The viewpoints of the English-speaking minority of Quebec were (and still are) sharply contrasted with the French Quebec perspective in the matter of language. In spite of the objections raised by the English-speaking minority of Quebec, in spite of the tendency of two French-speaking Quebecers out of ten to agree with these objections, and in spite of some disapproval of the 1977 Charter of the French Language,* it is clear that the majority in Quebec is united behind the objective of preserving and extending the use of the French language in Quebec. This objective is related, in the view of French-speaking political leaders, to the paramount objective of national survival.

Another objective pursued by French-speaking Quebecers relates to regional economic development. The inhabitants of Quebec are particularly dissatisfied with the state of their economy. They perceive themselves as being exploited by English-speaking managers, and they see the federal government as ignoring Quebec's economic interests. Although linguistic discrimination cannot explain much of Quebec's

---

* As revealed by the Goldfarb survey published September 26, 1977, in the Southam dailies. See *The Gazette*, Montreal, September 26, 1977, page 1. The data published by the Southam papers were somewhat contradicted by a survey commissioned by the *Reader's Digest*, October 1977.

Some 15 years before the American Revolution, the French colony of Quebec was conquered by British troops. That conquest deprived our society of a great many of its elite, who went back to France, and it turned over our political and economic life to foreign leadership.

The small Québécois community immediately became a very delicate plant, tenuously rooted in an alien and not always hospitable environment. Every effort had to be made to ensure its protection and even its survival. So the Quebec people instinctively retreated into their shells. And then it would take some 12 generations to bring us to the threshold of national maturity.

Of all the European groups who settled in America in the 17th century—French, Spanish, Portuguese and British—only the French have not yet attained full political autonomy.

But now, at long last, Quebec is a fully developed society. It has over six million people, 82 per cent of whom are French by descent, language and cultural heritage. Montreal, our metropolis, is the second largest French city in the world.

Our gross national product would make us 23rd among the nations of the world, and 11th on a per capita basis. And as for our territory, its store of resources is even more ample than its quite sufficient size.

Independence for Quebec, therefore, now appears as normal, I might say almost as inevitable, as it was for the American states of 200 years ago.

René Lévesque, speaking in New York, January 25, 1977.
Source: *The Gazette*, Montreal, January 26, 1977, p. 7.

economic lag behind New York State or Ontario, French-speaking Quebecers tend to put a great deal of emphasis on this factor. On the whole, French-speaking Quebecers would like to see the Quebec government foster the industrial development of Quebec, especially outside Montreal, to the benefit of French-speaking entrepreneurs, managers and workers.

A third objective on which one finds a large degree of agreement concerns the control that French-speaking Quebecers should exert over the political institutions which operate in Quebec. Many Quebecers tend to consider Quebec their homeland and they feel a loyalty to the

Quebec government and to the territorial symbols of Quebec. This loyalty outweighs the loyalty felt toward the federal government and the territorial symbols of Canada. In spite of their dual loyalties and all the ambiguities such divided loyalties can nourish, most French-speaking Quebecers favor an extension of the powers of the Quebec government—in other words, some kind of "devolution" from the federal government to the government of Quebec.

Survey data published in April 1977 showed that 33 per cent of the French-speaking Quebecers were already willing to go along with the Parti Québécois as far as "souveraineté-association". Another survey, published by the *Reader's Digest* in October 1977, showed that the proportion of those who support "souveraineté-association" has grown substantially, reaching the 38 per cent mark in the whole of Quebec and 44 per cent as far as Francophones alone are concerned.*

In sum, these objectives, which would result in increased autonomy, perhaps going as far as "souveraineté-association", are what a majority of Quebec voters want. Quebec is trying to become as French as the rest of Canada is English, in order to safeguard the French-speaking community, in order to insure the survival of French. Quebec is trying to give its government all the powers required to develop Quebec industry and foster economic progress for the French-speaking population. There is indeed a majority united behind these objectives, but this majority is not consolidated under a single political leadership. Most of it supports the Parti Québécois, while parts of it are scattered among the other parties.

---

* The answers to the question relating to "souveraineté-association" were, for the whole of Quebec, 38 per cent for, 44 per cent against, 18 per cent undecided; and, for Francophones alone, 44 per cent for, 37 per cent against, 19 per cent undecided. The *Reader's Digest* based its survey on a 823-person sample. This study is recommended reading. See *Reader's Digest*, October 1977, pages 55ff.

Notes to Part I

1. Bernard Smith, *La Loi 22* (Montreal: Editions du Jour, 1975), pages 58, 77, 79-86.
2. Claude Ryan, "*Le Devoir* et les minorités d'ici," *Le Devoir*, April 30, 1977, page 4.
3. Raymond Barbeau, *Le Québec est-il une colonie?* (Montreal: Les éditions de l'homme, 1962), page 144 (my translation).
4. See André d'Allemagne, *Le colonialisme au Québec* (Montreal: Editions R-B, 1966) or Raymond Barbeau, *Le Québec est-il une colonie?* (Montreal: Les éditions de l'homme, 1962).
5. Comité Canada, *Le séparatisme? Non! 100 fois non!* (Montreal: Les presses libres, 1970).
6. Jacques Henripin, "From Acceptance of Nature to Control: The Demography of the French Canadians since the Seventeenth Century," in Marcel Rioux and Yves Martin, *French-Canadian Society* (Toronto: McClelland and Stewart, 1964), vol. 1, page 210.
7. See *Comptes économiques du Québec* (Quebec: Ministry of Industry and Commerce, April 1, 1977).
8. These figures are shown by the surveys in the following texts: Mildred A. Schwartz, *Politics and Territory—The Sociology of Regional Persistence in Canada* (Montreal: McGill-Queen's University Press, 1971), pages 104, 125; Vincent Lemieux, Marcel Gilbert and André Blais, *Une élection de réalignement—L'élection générale du 29 avril 1970 au Québec* (Montreal: Editions du Jour, 1970), pages 90-93; Jane Jenson and Peter Regenstreif, "Some Dimensions of Partisan Choice in Quebec, 1969," *Canadian Jour-*

nal of Political Science/Revue canadienne de science politique, vol. III, no. 2 (June 1970), pages 308-317.

9. For example, see Raymond Barbeau, *J'ai choisi l'indépendance* (Montreal: Les éditions de l'homme, 1961), pages 34-35.

10. This has been documented in David J. Elkins and Richard Simeon, "Regional Political Culture in Canada," *Canadian Journal of Political Science/Revue canadienne de science politique*, vol. VII, no. 3 (September 1974), page 406.

11. A good example of this is *Québec, le coût de l'indépendance*, a study by the Chamber of Commerce of the Province of Quebec (Montreal: Editions du Jour, 1969).

12. *La Presse*, July 13, 1974, page A-5.

13. A chronology of the autonomist idea in Quebec is available in Robert Rumilly, *L'autonomie provinciale* (Montreal: Editions de l'arbre, 1948).

14. One particularly articulate description of the advantages of federalism can be found in Gilles Lalande, *Pourquoi le fédéralisme?: Contribution d'un Québécois a l'intelligence du fédéralisme canadien* (Montreal: Hurtubise/HMH, 1972).

15. Ibid., pages 21, 27, 169.

PART II: HOW?

Introduction

Even though a majority in Quebec agrees on the long-term general objectives of French language survival, increased economic well-being and preservation of the Quebec homeland, they are still divided on the *how*—the appropriate means to realize these objectives.

In the 1976 Quebec election campaign, the six major Quebec political parties were in favor of at least some extension of the French language in Quebec. The smallest of these six parties, the Democratic Alliance, led by Nick Auf der Maur, stated the minimum position: "French should be promoted in the business and cultural life of Quebec through encouragement, consultation and incentives, not through fear and coercion." The Alliance had 13 candidates in constituencies with large English-speaking populations, and it polled 17,444 votes (4.8 per cent of the votes in these 13 constituencies and fewer than half of one per cent of the 3,360,785 votes cast in the election).

A still smaller party, the Quebec New Democratic Party (which polled 3,101 votes with 21 candidates (fewer than 0.3 per cent of the votes polled in the 21 districts) held the following position:

> Schools in Quebec should be French: schools should speak the language of more than 80 per cent of the population. French is the general rule.
>
> After a transition period during which no student already enrolled will be obliged to change schools, the linguistic minorities in Quebec will attend the common schools. Where the need and the desire are felt, courses in minority languages will be available, but without ever calling into question the quality and the integrity of the instruction in French.

We commit ourselves to defending the recognition of French as the language of work and the sole official language of Quebec.[1]

The positions of the Democratic Alliance (10 of whose 13 candidates had English as their mother tongue) and of the Quebec New Democratic Party (five of whose 21 candidates had English as their mother tongue) are interesting primarily because of the high proportion of English-speaking candidates and party workers in their organizations. These two were the only parties in which English-speaking candidates and party workers were overrepresented in comparison with the 18 per cent that English-speaking Quebecers constitute in Quebec's population. In each of the other parties, English-speaking Quebecers made up less than 15 per cent of the candidates and party workers. On the language issue, all these parties (Liberals, Créditistes, Parti Québécois, Union Nationale, Parti National Populaire, and smaller parties) took positions that were, in general, as strong as that of the Quebec New Democratic Party.

In four parties, which polled a total of 65 per cent of the votes, references to the idea of a "nation" were commonplace in speeches and texts devoted to the language question and to constitutional problems. The Union Nationale is clearly identified with this idea, the very term "Union Nationale" having been, from the start in 1935, a reference to the French-Canadian nation. The Parti National Populaire has also chosen to refer to the idea of a "nation" in its name. The leader of the Quebec Créditistes (Social Credit), Camil Samson, spoke of the "nation canadienne-française" on numerous occasions. As for the Parti Québécois, its nationalist stand is well known.

The other parties, including the Quebec Liberal party, made very few references to the idea of a "nation". Such expressions as "nation canadienne", "nation canadienne-française", "nation québécoise", and the qualification "national" were rarely used and, indeed, these formulas have been taken out of Liberal party literature. Nevertheless, the Liberal leader, Robert Bourassa, often resorted to formulas such as "société québécoise", "les Québécois" and "tous les Québécois".

The first objective, the survival of the French language, or, in the view of a majority, the survival of a French-speaking "nation" or "society" is supported by every political party represented in the Quebec National Assembly (and one can note that the Quebec legislature is known as a *National* Assembly).

The second major objective, economic development, is also of paramount importance in the platform of every political party in Quebec. However, in the economic sector, there seem to be four distinct views on *how* this economic development should be achieved. The first and least significant of these views is held by the small parties of the left, none of which polled more than half of one per cent of the votes in the 1976 election.* These small parties favor a socialist solution to the economic problems of Quebec, but a very mild one compared with the solutions put forward by their counterparts in European countries. The members of these small parties of the left talk a lot about "class conflict", "bourgeoisie", "proletariat", "capitalism", "exploitation of the working class", and "imperialism". Their programs include proposals to nationalize the Bell Telephone Company and some corporations where labor problems have been acute.

A different view on economic development is held by the Parti Québécois. That party, in spite of its reliance on government intervention for economic development, does not talk of nationalization (except in the case of asbestos). On the contrary, Parti Québécois leaders have always advocated an increase in government aid to improve the productivity of Quebec's small and medium-sized enterprises and co-operatives, which together employ half the work force. The Parti Québécois does not challenge the maintenance of the economic system based as it is on private enterprise and the market, but it emphasizes the role of the government which it sees as a promoter of economic development and not solely as a caretaker of the economy. Moreover, the Parti Québécois believes strongly in small and medium-sized enterprises and co-operatives, which it sees as a source of ideas, goodwill, and progress.

The economic platform of the Parti Québécois differs considerably from the programs of the left-wing parties and is far from being "socialist" (in the Marxist meaning of the term). This economic platform, however, is "socially-minded" and it shows a bias in favor of

* The Democratic Alliance, led by Nick Auf der Maur, could be classified as one of the small parties of the left. However its program cannot be termed socialist: it is progressive. The Democratic Alliance opposes French unilingualism and Quebec sovereignty and, in November 1976, it stood against the Parti Québécois on these grounds. The Democratic Alliance also condemns spending extravaganzas, low political morality, and regressive government action, and, in 1976, it offered an "alternative" to the English-speaking voters with this platform.

enterprise controlled by French-speaking Quebec. Finally, by empha-
sizing government action (tax incentives, government purchasing policies, regionalization of government operations, and so on), the Parti
Québécois of necessity supports greater economic powers for the
Quebec government.

The third view of how Quebec economic development should be
achieved is held by the Quebec Liberal party. The Liberals put their
emphasis on larger companies and on giant projects which they see as
the greatest levers of economic progress. They also favor increased
activity in Montreal and in Quebec City, because they believe the
development of these centres will induce the development of their
periphery and hinterland much better than any sprinkling of government grants and subsidies to remote areas could do. The Quebec
Liberal party welcomes foreign investment. It does not favor massive
government intervention, especially at the provincial level where economic powers are limited. Such views are compatible with the objectives of the Montreal business community and with the views held by
many "liberal" economists such as André Raynauld. The views of the
Quebec Liberal party on the economic development of Quebec do not
challenge the interests of the larger corporations and they do not
require any constitutional change in order to be implemented.

The fourth view on the means to achieve the economic development
of Quebec is held by the three political parties based in the rural and
semi-rural areas of Quebec: the Union Nationale, led by Rodrigue
Biron in the Quebec election of 1976, the Ralliement Créditiste, led by
Camil Samson, and the Parti National Populaire, represented by
Fabien Roy in the Quebec National Assembly after the 1976 election.
These three small parties, which accounted for 24 per cent of the votes
cast in 1976, favor small and medium-sized enterprises, and they favor
some government action in the areas of agriculture, mines, forests,
fisheries and tourism. They would like to see more processing of
Quebec's natural resources done in Quebec. These planks are similar
to those of the Parti Québécois on the same questions. The three
"rural" parties, however, condemn the "excessive" reliance placed by
the Parti Québécois on government intervention. At the same time,
they do not agree with the Quebec Liberal party on such matters as
Montreal-based economic development.

Although such a concise presentation of the economic platforms of
the political parties that competed in the Quebec 1976 election cannot
fully reflect the variety of the proposals put forward, it summarizes the

Table 5—Main Views of Quebec Political Parties on Economic Development

Parties	Degree of Government Intervention	Territorial Emphasis	Preferred Economic Agent	Constitutional Changes Required in the Economic Sector	Percentage of Vote in 1976
Left-Wing Parties*	Medium to extreme	None	Public enterprise	Varying	1% (total)
Parti Québécois	Large	Quebec regions	Public enterprise small and medium-sized enterprises, co-operatives	Large	41%
Quebec Liberal Party	Medium	Quebec industrial centers	Large corporations	Little or None	34%
Union Nationale, Ralliement Créditste, Parti National Populaire	Small	Quebec regions	Small and medium-sized enterprises	Some	24% (total)

essentials. In a capsule, the four main views held by the political parties of Quebec on its economic development are set out in table 5.

In spite of the very significant differences in the economic programs of the Quebec political parties, all parties agree that Quebec economic development is a fundamental objective. Quebec is no different from

* These left-wing parties were those which had at least one known candidate in the 1976 election: Groupe Marxiste Revolutionnaire, Ligue Socialiste Ouvrière, Ligue Communiste, Parti Communiste, Parti Ouvrier, Parti des Travailleurs, Coalition des Militant Syndicaux et Nouveau Parti Democratique. The Democratic Alliance platform does not fit the above classification, and its stands on the various issues would call for a separate category altogether.

other areas of Canada or the rest of the western world in this regard. What is different in Quebec is the view held by many that this economic objective cannot be achieved without constitutional change.

Whether they believe that constitutional amendments are required or not, the spokesmen for the five political parties represented in the Quebec National Assembly in 1976 (both before and after the November election) all agreed on the idea of giving the Quebec government substantially increased powers, at least in the socio-cultural domain. The differences among the parties regarding the third basic objective of making Quebec the homeland of French-speaking Canadians relate to the degree or importance of the transfers from Ottawa to Quebec that are required; they do not relate to the idea itself. It is the idea of a homeland for the French-speaking Quebecers that necessitates constitutional adjustments. And constitutional adjustments appear to be the stumbling block against which Quebec comes to grief.

4

Political Sovereignty

The most far-reaching constitutional change proposed by a Quebec political party represented in the Quebec National Assembly is "sovereignty-association", that is a transfer to the Quebec government of all constitutional powers currently held by the federal government, followed or accompanied by the establishment of decision-making mechanisms in the economic sector controlled jointly by the governments of Quebec and Canada. As it is explained by Parti Québécois spokesmen, "sovereignty-association" would free Quebec from the traditional century-old federalism under which Canada has lived since 1867 and introduce into Canada the kind of federalism which is gradually being installed in Europe.

In 1970, the program of the Parti Québécois was titled *La Solution*, and after 15 years of debate within Quebec about the "ideal" constitutional arrangement, the "sovereignty-association" proposal seemed as if it really might be the solution. It could rally those Quebec nationalists who had argued for all-out Quebec independence as well as those who had called for increased Quebec autonomy. It had, by 1970, already gone a long way toward healing the historic division of nationalist forces in Quebec and had the support of most nationalist organizations. It was consistent with the basic objectives shared by a large proportion of French-speaking Quebecers: survival of the French language and of a French "nation" in Quebec, along with economic development for the benefit of the Quebec population. And it seemed to offer "national dignity" through control by the Quebec population of political institutions operating in Quebec.

The leaders of the Parti Québécois continue to believe that their solution will rally a near-unanimity of French-speaking Quebecers and even a substantial proportion of bilingual Quebecers of British origin whose roots in Quebec go back several generations. They hold the conviction that Quebec would fare far better in every aspect of its cultural, social and economic life, if the Quebec government controlled all the taxes levied in Quebec and was solely responsible for public administration. The main argument of Parti Québécois leaders such as Jacques Parizeau is just that:

> Quebecers have full control over the Quebec government and the Quebec government is the only government over which Quebecers have full control, and if it were the only government to operate in Quebec, Quebecers could have policies appropriate to their needs and a guarantee of efficiency and dynamism in public administration.

Some Parti Québécois leaders even argue that their solution will rally a large proportion of English-speaking Canadians living outside Quebec.* They cite several factors favoring this development. First, many English-speaking Canadians would be relieved to see that policies suited to their own needs could henceforth be defined without reference to the different needs of Quebec and without being eroded by compromises. Second, the Parti Québécois solution would save millions of dollars now spent in translation, debating, negotiation and conflicts caused by the presence of the federal government in Quebec.** Third, the Parti Québécois solution would bring about the end of federal equalization payments to Quebec, which amount to more than one billion dollars annually and are seen as a sop to Quebec although, according to Claude Morin, they are paid for by Quebec taxpayers.[2] Finally, many Parti Québécois leaders think that English-speaking Canadians, freed from the "Quebec problem", would get a chance to progress in their own way, building their nation.

* Gallup poll data published by the weekly supplement *The Canadian* (circulation 2,500,000) , on April 9, 1977, revealed that 44.8 per cent of English-speaking respondents answered "yes" to the following question: "If separation occurs, should Canada enter into an economic union with Quebec?", while 39.0 per cent said "no" and 15.9 per cent did not state an opinion. The representative sample was made up of 1,043 adult Canadians.

** In 1975, there were 1,400 translators in the federal government translation bureau. The costs expected in 1980 were $60 million (1975 dollars). See *Fifth Annual Report of the Commissioner of Official Languages* (Ottawa: Information Canada, 1976), p. 150.

We therefore propose a new type of association with the rest of Canada, a set of new ties so that both nations, the English and the French, may live in harmony, side by side, without hurting each other. That we stand ready to discuss at any time, with our minds open to pooling or "joint-venturing" whatever should be if both Quebec and Canada are to profit from and with one another.

This new partnership could take the form, essentially, of a common market based on a customs union, permitting free passage of persons, goods and capital, as in the countries of Western Europe.

Additionally, if the desire is mutual, we are ready to go further, as far as monetary union, which obviously would allow for political change to be implemented with a real minimum of uncertainty in economic affairs . . .

And as for labeling our program, if it's necessary, we can call it "social democratic". Social democratic parties have been, or are presently in power in several western countries of some importance, like Sweden, Great Britain, West Germany, and also in certain Canadian provinces . . .

Our model, so to speak, for social and economic development is based on respect for the individual and on keeping people well informed about and involved in all major decisions that concern them. We want fully responsible citizens.

René Lévesque, speaking in New York, January 25, 1977.
Source: *The Gazette*, Montreal, January 26, 1977, p. 7.

Independence

The solution put forward by the Parti Québécois has been described in a series of documents, among which the best known have been *Option Québec*, a book written by René Lévesque which appeared in January 1968; *La Solution*, the 1970 booklet summarizing the party program; and *Un Gouvernement du Parti Québécois s'engage*, the 1973 summary of the program.

The last document published before the 1976 election was entitled: *Le programme, l'action politique, les statuts et reglements, Edition 1975, Parti Québécois*. This document states the various objectives set by the party's fifth national convention in November 1974; it outlines how a Parti Québécois government would bring about Quebec independence, describes how an independent Quebec would run its foreign relations and states the party's objectives in the domestic sector. In spite of its importance, this document has not been issued for general distribution, although it was made available to every Parti Québécois member and to any person who asked for it. Some 200,000 copies had been put into circulation by the end of 1976. During the 1976 election campaign the Parti Québécois published small booklets and pamphlets which were consistent with this program, instead of a summary of the program itself.

The solution proposed by the Parti Québécois, sovereignty for Quebec and economic association between Quebec and Canada, has not been modified substantially since 1968. The main change in the party's platform was made in 1974 when the party convention adopted a resolution on the procedure to be used to ascertain the existence of a majority of Quebec voters in support of the Parti Québécois solution. Instead of considering a Parti Québécois election victory as sufficient proof of support for Quebec independence, the 1974 convention decided to distinguish between an election for seats in the National Assembly and a referendum on Quebec independence. People could thus vote for Parti Québécois candidates in a general election without necessarily voting for independence. As Parti Québécois propagandists had already stated during the 1973 election campaign: "First things first. Today I vote to form a government. Later, by referendum, I will decide on Quebec's future."

This recourse to a referendum was justified from the point of view of democracy as well as that of pure partisanship. With Quebec's single-member constituency system, it could—and eventually did—happen that the Parti Québécois would get a majority of seats in the National Assembly with fewer than 50 per cent of the votes. The leaders of the Parti Québécois considered that Quebec independence was too serious a project to undertake without the democratic support of an absolute majority of Quebec voters. Consequently, they felt that the policy of "accession to independence by steps" had to be introduced. But to distinguish between the election of a government and a referendum on Quebec independence was also good strategy. It could and did help defuse the propaganda of opposing parties, which were likely to equate a vote for the Parti Québécois with a vote for economic chaos, labelled "separatism".

During the 1976 election campaign, Parti Québécois spokesmen made skilful use of their promise to hold a referendum on Quebec independence. When asked about their party's independence proposal, René Lévesque and other Parti Québécois candidates systematically replied that there would be plenty of time for a debate on independence, because a referendum was to be held in due time. If pressed for more details, Lévesque and his colleagues would add: "Read the program; it is available upon request at the party office."

The program included the following plank: "A Parti Québécois Government is pledged to put into effect Quebec political *sovereignty* through democratic processes and to propose to Canada a mutually beneficial economic *association*."[3] The reference to the proposed referendum reads as follows:

> The right of peoples to self-determination, that is their right to choose their own political regime, is inscribed in the Charter of the United Nations, to which Canada itself has adhered, along with more than 130 other countries. International law and custom provide the mechanisms by which peoples can accede to political sovereignty. Besides, since Quebecers, like their Canadian and American neighbors, live under a democratic regime, it is the people, in this type of regime, who hold the power to decide by means of the vote. It is thus by this democratic process accepted by all that Quebec, after an election, will realize its political sovereignty, while maintaining with its neighbors and with other countries friendly relations based on respect for international law.

> Therefore, **a Parti Québécois government pledges:**

> **1.** To set in motion, immediately, the process of accession to sovereignty by proposing to the National Assembly, soon after its election, a law authorizing it:
>
> **a)** to demand from Ottawa the repatriation to Quebec of all powers except those which the two governments want to entrust to common organizations for the purpose of economic association;
>
> **b)** to undertake, with the view of attaining this objective, technical discussions with Ottawa on the arranged transfer of powers;
>
> **c)** to work out with Canada agreements touching especially on the division of assets and liabilities as well as of public

property, in conformity with the usual rules of international law.

2. If it should become necessary to proceed unilaterally, to assume methodically the exercise of all the powers of a sovereign state, having ensured beforehand that it has the support of the Quebec people by means of a referendum.[4]

René Lévesque and his ministers have talked so much about the proposed referendum that Quebec voters have no reason to fear a unilateral declaration of independence on the part of the Parti Québécois government without such a referendum having been held and won by the pro-independence forces.

Would the Parti Québécois Settle for Less?

Has the Parti Québécois any chance to win a referendum proposing Quebec political sovereignty in an economic association with Canada? If it lost the referendum, would the Parti Québécois settle for a compromise such as special status for Quebec? And if there were a compromise, what would be the reaction of the die-hard "indépendantistes"? These are some of the questions which concern federal ministers and civil servants as well as other Canadians. The answers to such questions can only be obtained with time; however, intentions can be studied, and they provide some indications about the future.

Every statement uttered by Parti Québécois leaders reveals that they are determined to achieve their aim: Quebec political sovereignty. They have already studied and rejected many other proposals, notably those put forward by the Union Nationale in 1966 and by the promoters of special status. They have been fighting for Quebec political sovereignty for 10 long years. Many members of the Parti Québécois were "indépendantistes" as early as 1960 and some of them have put in long hours over a period of years working for independence parties. These people *know*—and it is more than faith—they *know* that Quebec, one day, will be a sovereign, separate country, which they hope will be linked to Canada through some kind of confederal arrangement, be it a monetary union or a free-trade association.

Parti Québécois leaders *know* there will be a majority of Quebec voters in favor of their solution, in the 1980s at the latest. This conviction is based on demographic trends in the Quebec electorate.

The independence idea was first propagated by Quebec teachers, artists, poets, novelists, singers, journalists and other "intellectual workers" who, by 1966, were either converted to the idea or at least not actively opposed to it. The support given by the intellectual avant-garde to independence was illustrated by a survey published in a weekend newspaper on November 13, 1976: more than 100 Quebec television and radio artists (including Monique Leyrac, Jean Duceppe and George Dor) stated, by name, that they supported the Parti Québécois. Among the 147 artists who said how they would vote, 142 were in favor of the Parti Québécois.[5]

The intellectual "avant-garde" was joined in the mid-1960s by the students at Quebec's colleges and universities. In 1966, these two groups constituted the bulk of the independence forces. By 1970 they had been joined by older nationalists (such as René Lévesque and other former Quebec Liberals) and by members of the trade unions (particularly some of their advisers such as Robert Burns and Charles Tremblay). In 1970, the Parti Québécois had a majority in the 18-24 age group; in 1973, it had a majority in the 18-30 age group; in 1976, it had a majority in the 18-35 age group. In 1980, if the trend is maintained, it will have a majority in the 18-40 age group, and probably also in the 40-45 age group, with a good showing (40 per cent) in the 45-55 category: this will make for a solid and absolute majority of the whole Quebec electorate.

On November 15, 1976, the Parti Québécois won the votes of some 50 per cent of French-speaking Quebec voters. Among French-speaking voters who have 12 or more years of schooling, 70 per cent supported the Parti Québécois. And, according to both polls and Parti Québécois surveys, more than 20 per cent of bilingual English Quebec voters supported the Parti Québécois. But the Parti Québécois got nothing from unilingual English Quebec voters and very little from older voters, in spite of a lot of campaigning among older voters in east-end Montreal.

Surveys have shown that the Parti Québécois generally retains the support of those who have voted for its candidates once. A Gallup poll published in the Montreal daily *La Presse* on May 2, 1976, estimated that 81 per cent of those who had voted for the Parti Québécois in 1973 were still supporting it three years later. This conclusion was supported by the study carried out by sociologists Maurice Pinard and Richard Hamilton in November 1976. But support for the Parti Québécois does not necessarily imply approval for its sovereignty proposal. In the November 1976 study, Pinard and Hamilton showed that only half of those who voted for the Parti Québécois were also in favor of "Quebec becoming an independent (separate) country."*

Commentators often state that the proportion of Quebec voters who support the idea of an independent Quebec hovers around 15 per cent and is stationary. The fact is that between 1962 and 1967, surveys which included a question on Quebec independence registered on the average nine per cent in favor, 75 per cent against, and 14 per cent abstaining. Support for the independence parties in the 1966 election was very close to the nine per cent figure. Surveys done between 1967 and 1972 showed that the average support for Quebec independence had climbed to 11 per cent (or 13 per cent if only French-speaking voters were considered). In the period 1972-1977, the average support reached 17 per cent (or 22 per cent if only French-speaking voters are considered). Members of the Parti Québécois who have studied both published and unpublished data contend that, if a referendum were held in 1978, the support for "Quebec political sovereignty in an economic association with Canada" would reach *at least* 40 per cent of the votes cast (that is 30 per cent of Quebec voters would vote yes, 45 per cent would vote no, and 25 per cent would abstain). The proportion of those who approve of Quebec independence certainly does not stand at 15 per cent of Quebec voters: it has been increasing gradually and it is probably closer to the Parti Québécois figures than to the 1965 statistics which are so often quoted.**

Support for Quebec independence has gradually increased with time, and, in my view, it is likely to increase further, because of the demographic trends which favor the Parti Québécois and because of the greater propaganda effort that can be put behind the idea now that the Parti Québécois is the Quebec government.

In other words, the Parti Québécois does have a chance of winning a referendum held in 1980 or after on the question of "Quebec political sovereignty in an economic association with Canada."

* Reference to this study has been made above.

** The CBC *Sunday Morning* survey of April 3, 1977, showed that 32 per cent of the respondents approved of "souveraineté-association," but only 16 per cent approved of "souveraineté" *without* "association". The survey data published in October 1977 by the *Reader's Digest* and based on a sample of 823 Quebecers, showed that the proportion had climbed to 40 per cent in the case of those who approved of "souveraineté-association," while 19 per cent approved of "independence" (without association).

However, if the referendum were forced upon the Parti Québécois earlier than its strategists consider desirable, it could well be that a majority would say no to independence. Would the Parti Québécois then settle for a compromise?

As far as I can judge from personal acquaintance with some members of the Parti Québécois, from interviews with party activists and from available public statements, the Parti Québécois sees political sovereignty as the prerequisite for achieving the fundamental objectives of the French-speaking population of Quebec (survival as a "nation", economic development, and so on). Full political sovereignty implies the following transfers of powers from Ottawa to Quebec: taxation, foreign affairs and defence, agriculture, communications, energy, mines, resources, justice, labor, corporate affairs, citizenship, immigration—indeed, every area of government jurisdiction except those specifically related to economic union.

However, the degree of association, in the view of many, could be pushed as far as a full economic union. Economic union is a "federal" arrangement in which the participating units maintain their sovereignty while agreeing to harmonize their taxation and social policies, to use one common currency, to use one common tariff and to practise free trade within their common boundaries. The "central" institutions in an economic union normally include a central bank, an economic council, a tariff commission, and a series of joint committees, some of them with large secretariats, research staffs and statistical services.

If the compromise offered to Quebec by Canada were to take the form of an economic union (which is more than a monetary union, much more than a common market, and very much more than a free-trade association), it is safe to predict that it would be accepted. If the proposed compromise were to exclude full political sovereignty for Quebec, it is safe to predict that it would be rejected by the Parti Québécois which would instead wait another few years until the time was ripe for its own referendum.

At this point, it is too early for any political leader to dare say that Canadians could come up with a compromise making Quebec politically sovereign within a Quebec-Canada economic union. This makes it hard to predict whether such a compromise is possible. The reaction of die-hard Quebec "indépendantistes" to this compromise is also very difficult to predict, although many believe that it would be accepted. In addition, many events affect the path of history, and it could well be that the Quebec independence movement will falter as a result of such unexpected contingencies as the death of a leader, a leadership crisis, a change in political personnel, a severe economic setback, a sudden oil discovery, pressures from outside or other events beyond its control.

Arguments for Quebec Political Sovereignty: The International Aspect

Although the Parti Québécois has made French the official language of Quebec and the compulsory language of instruction for immigrants and immigrants' children, many party members believe that this is not sufficient. What is needed, in their view, is a clear understanding that Quebec is a sovereign country, distinct from Canada although associated with it in economic matters. Only if they know that Quebec is a sovereign country will immigrants join Quebec's French-speaking society. If they consider Quebec a "province" in an English-speaking country, immigrants settling in Montreal will continue to behave as they have in the past. They will integrate or try to integrate into the economically dominant English-speaking community. In the long run, in spite of the Charter of the French Language, immigrants settling in Quebec and their children will become English-speaking Quebecers. Many members of the Parti Québécois believe that the government of Canada has long been trying to submerge French-speaking Quebecers under a flood of immigrants, just as the colonial administrations did between 1840 and 1867.

In this view, French-speaking Quebecers, who have now entered the industrial age, can no longer count on high fertility rates and rural isolation in their fight for national or cultural survival. They require full control over immigration policies so that their society will not be overrun by English-speaking immigrants. From this point of view, legislative powers over immigration and citizenship must be transferred to Quebec. Advocates of this argument still favor immigration if it serves to strengthen Quebec's French-speaking society. In order to get would-be immigrants from other countries to come to Quebec knowing that Quebec is a French-speaking country, the Quebec government needs the power to open embassies in foreign capitals. These embassies would make Quebec known abroad and would cater to the needs of potential immigrants to Quebec. In order to have embassies abroad, Quebec needs recognition as a politically sovereign country, with full control over foreign affairs and an international status.

The argument for full control over foreign affairs is based on other needs as well. In order to foster its economic and cultural development, Quebec needs the capacity to enter into exchanges with other countries, especially those which have things in common with Quebec in terms of either language or cultural heritage. People who speak Spanish, Portuguese, Italian or Greek, as well as French-speaking people, are most often mentioned in this context.

Some of these international exchanges favored by Parti Québécois members are of an altruistic nature. Quebecers who are internationally-minded are particularly numerous in the Parti Québécois and they believe that Quebec could have useful ties with the French-speaking African countries and some of the Spanish-speaking nations, not to set the stage for a new North American economic imperialism but to help them overcome their economic and political dependency.

Parti Québécois leaders would also like to see more international exchanges in the cultural domain. In 1974, Quebec held a "Super-franco-fête" to which delegations from a dozen African countries were invited. This event was an eye-opener for many Quebecers, who became convinced of the benefits which accrue from such international ventures. In the same vein, Quebec and France have had exchanges of students, artists, teachers and technicians, among others, since 1967. The benefits are not measured in dollars but in life experiences, and they are viewed as being well worth the money. Quebecers want to expand these international exchanges, and it would be easier to do so if Quebec had control over foreign affairs.

But the international exchanges which Parti Québécois members favor most strongly fall in the economic sector. Quebec needs to sell its products abroad; it needs new markets. In its trade, Canada has traditionally favored English-speaking countries, and particularly the United Kingdom and the United States.* Less than one per cent of Canada's foreign trade, for instance, is with France, which is a market of 50 million people. Quebecers who favor political sovereignty think that if only one quarter of the Canadian external affairs budget had been managed by Quebec, Quebec would be far better off today.

These arguments, and many others which have to do with deeper nationalist feelings, have led the Parti Québécois to include the following statement in the *Programme*:

* About 69 to 72 per cent of Canada's international trade is with the United States, and between four and six per cent of Canada's exports go to the United Kingdom. Japan accounts for six to seven per cent of Canada's trade.

A Parti Québécois government pledges:

. . . to seek Quebec's admission to the United Nations and to obtain recognition from other countries

. . . to respect, among the treaties binding Canada, those which are favorable to Quebec, and to follow international law in the renunciation of other treaties

. . . to pursue a foreign policy of peaceful co-operation.[6]

These preliminary statements are elaborated in a long section of the program devoted to Quebec foreign policy and defence. The preamble to this section states that Quebecers in the 1970s want to participate fully in the world outside. They conceive of their foreign policy as being the implementation of two main principles: 1) the safeguarding of the interests of the Quebec people, peace, security and the necessity of interdependence and economic and socio-cultural ties with other states; and 2) the solidarity of the Quebec people with developing peoples.

The whole section is worth quoting at length:

A Parti Québécois government pledges:

1. To promote the liberty of peoples and respect for their national character along with international co-operation based on justice, progress and peace; to reject all forms of neo-colonialism in international relations, notably by supervising the investments and the behavior of Quebec companies in foreign countries; to avoid co-operation with any regime that does not respect the Human Rights Charter of the United Nations.

2. To respect the principle of non-interference in the internal affairs of another state.

3. To establish ties of co-operation and goodwill with the international community, while considering as priorities:

a) the replacement of preferential ties with the Commonwealth by close relations with French-speaking countries;

b) the establishment of relations with the countries of the Third World, especially those of Latin America;

c) the close ties that link us with Canada and the United States of America.

4. To open up a number, limited at first, of diplomatic missions and consulates, the heads of which could be accredited to several countries or international bodies.

5. To practise a pacifist foreign policy based on the rejection of the recourse to war as a solution to international differences, disarmament, the banning of the testing and use of nuclear and bacteriological weapons, and withdrawal from military alliances such as NORAD and NATO. [This last phrase was removed during the Parti Québécois convention May 29, 1977.]

6. To reduce military expenditures substantially by substituting for traditional armed forces territorial defence units which could be available for non-military purposes and could collaborate with the United Nations in its peacekeeping missions.

7. To create a research and supervision unit, responsible to the National Assembly, which would aim to eliminate political intervention by multinational corporations in the State of Quebec.*

In the area of economic relations with other countries, the Parti Québécois program states that:

A Parti Québécois government pledges:

... to respect the General Agreement on Tariffs and Trade (GATT), which anticipates a freeze or reduction of tariffs by a large number of countries and a renunciation of tariff increases.

... to respect international law in the formulation of our international economic policy.[7]

The options outlined in this section accurately reflect the opinions held by a majority of French-speaking Quebecers in the field of external affairs, as revealed by public opinion polls published since the end of World War II, and as shown by the behavior of Quebec voters in 1942 when Canada was asked, in a plebiscite, whether it favored military conscription for service abroad. According to many students of Canadian external affairs, until the 1970s the viewpoints of French Canada were systematically discarded by Canada's policy-makers

---

* *Le programme... Edition 1975*, pages 9 and 10, translation. The change in the earlier proposal to withdraw an independent Quebec from NORAD and NATO has developed since the Parti Québécois gained control of the Quebec government. The leaders of the Parti Québécois have made it clear that the proposed defence policy of the future sovereign Quebec is under study and that it is not now foreseen that Quebec should withdraw from NORAD and NATO. The statements uttered by the Parti Québécois leaders since November 15, 1976, are to the effect that Quebec is part of North America and that it shares responsibility in matters of defence.

In a referendum, the precise wording of the question is of relatively little significance.

Si vous voulez éviter la·conscriptiv.,

voici où vous ferez votre croix au plébiscite du 27 avril:

Consentez-vous à libérer le Gouvernement de toute obligation résultant d'engagements antérieurs restreignant les méthodes de mobilisation pour le service militaire ?	**OUI**
	NON X

The question put to the people of Canada on April 27, 1942 was ambiguous, but the opinion leaders made it clear enough by resorting to propaganda devices such as this damaged copy of a 1942 handbill, which was distributed all over Quebec. French-speaking Quebec stood four-square against conscription, and the *No* vote received an overwhelming majority in that province.

Source: *The Montreal Star*, April 30, 1977, page A-13.

when there were differences of opinion between French- and English-speaking Canadians in the area of foreign policy.

The Parti Québécois leaders favor free trade and increased economic exchanges with the eastern United States, Europe, Africa and South America. The leading economists of the Parti Québécois are known to have been supporters of free trade long before they joined the party. Rodrigue Tremblay, now Minister of Industry and Commerce, wrote a pamphlet in 1970 proposing a Quebec-United States common market.[8]

The Economic Aspect

According to a Parti Québécois election pamphlet entitled *Enough is*

Enough—The English and the '76 Election, one of Quebec's problems is
that the federal government does not protect Quebec industries:

> Look at the case of textiles. This is a gradually declining industry
> in Quebec and more and more workers are being laid off. Why?
> Because the Federal government insists on importing textiles from
> Korea, Hong Kong, and Taiwan in order to protect the sale of
> western Canadian wheat.
>
> Furthermore the government has failed to protect Quebec's
> dairy farmers from federal policies which reduced their incomes.
> These policies resulted in Quebec earning only 9% of Canadian
> agricultural revenues from some 27% of Canada's farming popula-
> tion.[9]

Such examples were used in 1976 by the Parti Québécois publicists
to convey the idea that federal policies have been detrimental to
Quebec economic development. Similar arguments were used in 1973
when, in a booklet entitled *Le coup du fédéralisme,* Parti Québécois
publicists strongly criticized federal policies in agriculture, labor, natural resources, scientific research and transport.

In the labor sector, the federal government has established policies
which are implemented by a Department of Labor, a Department of
Employment and Immigration, a Public Service Commission, an
Unemployment Insurance Commission, and several other federal institutions. The main Parti Québécois criticism of these policies, as
expressed in *Le coup du fédéralisme,* is that they account for several
thousands of jobs being offered in Ontario (particularly in Ottawa)
when they should be distributed over Canadian territory. In 1970,
according to *Le coup du fédéralisme,* 18,000 of these jobs should have
been located in Quebec, and the fact that they were not accounted for
a $200-million loss every year for Quebec taxpayers and the Quebec
economy.*

The other basic criticism is that these policies were built up to suit
the expansionist thrust of the federal civil service and were not
directed toward Quebec problems: they were band-aids on a broken
leg. According to *Le coup du fédéralisme,* federal mismanagement of
taxpayers' money spent in the labor sector accounted for a significant
portion of Quebec's excessively high unemployment rate. If only one

---

* Since 1968, the federal government's expansion on the Quebec side of
the federal capital region has indeed located 18,000 more jobs in
Quebec.

fifth of the money spent by the federal government in its labor programs had been spent by a Quebec government concerned about real Quebec problems, more than one billion dollars a year could have been pumped into the Quebec economy.[10] Therefore, the argument goes, Quebec needs full control over labor, employment, unemployment, and manpower policies and services.

In the field of natural resources, the federal government is accused of systematic unfairness to Quebec. In *Le coup du fédéralisme*, statistics were quoted showing that Quebec, with 28 per cent of Canada's population, received only 14 per cent of federal expenditures in the agricultural sector, eight per cent of federal expenditures in the sector of mines, forests and fisheries, five per cent under Canada's water programs, and two per cent under Canada's energy programs, for the years 1963-1968.[11] The conclusion was obvious: Quebec had to assume total jurisdiction in these areas.

The booklet was also very critical of the federal government's scientific research policies. It showed that in 1969-1970, to take one example, Ottawa spent $260 million on research in federal laboratories and research centres: of this, $13 million was spent in Quebec and $200 million in Ontario. Outside contracts to universities in 1970-1971 amounted to $132 million, but Quebec universities received only $23 million of this and Quebec French-speaking universities, $14 million (that is ten per cent of the total, when French-speaking Quebecers account for 23 per cent of the total Canadian population). The same proportions held true for grants and subsidies awarded to individuals. The conclusion, again, was obvious: Quebec had to get full control over government-funded scientific research.

The fourth domain on which *Le coup du fédéralisme* touched was transportation policies. It showed how federal investments in Quebec were insufficient and usually served the interests of other parts of Canada: three examples were railways (11 per cent of Canada's rail mileage is located in Quebec), seaports (those of Quebec have been neglected to the benefit of eastern ports and inland facilities on the Great Lakes), and aviation (the latest airport, Mirabel, having been conceived to serve Ottawa and Montreal, rather than Montreal and Quebec City.) Again the argument concluded that Quebec had no choice but to gain sovereignty in the domain of transportation.

The federal policies which stir the loudest criticism in Quebec, however, are policies over which the province could legislate under the British North America Act of 1867, if judicial interpretations were favorable. The provinces have jurisdiction over "public works", "municipalities", "hospitals", "education", "property and civil rights", "public lands and forests" and "local or private matters." But the Canadian Parliament has jurisdiction over every matter that does not fall under exclusive provincial jurisdiction.

Moreover, while the provinces can raise revenue by resorting to direct taxation in order to finance the implementation of provincial policies, the central government can raise revenue by any mode or system of taxation. Judicial interpretation has been that the federal government can resort to direct taxation, even though "direct taxation for provincial purposes" is a provincial jurisdiction. And the courts agree that the federal government can spend its money without any restriction on the object of its expenditure, because the only restrictions on spending in the British North America Act apply to the provinces, not to the central government.

Until 1976 when the Parti Québécois gained power, the interpretation of the British North America Act had always been the key issue. The provinces, for instance, have jurisdiction over hospitals (section 92, paragraph 7), except navy hospitals. Can the federal Parliament legislate in matters of health, a domain which is not mentioned in the British North America Act? The provinces have exclusive jurisdiction over municipal institutions (section 92, paragraph 8). Can the federal Parliament legislate on housing and on similar subjects which have traditionally been the concern of municipal institutions?

The answer to each of these questions and to all others concerning governmental jursidictions has generally been yes—the federal government can enter sectors on which the British North America Act is unclear, either by means of legislation or by means of administrative and budgetary action. If an activity were neither foreseen nor allocated to any government in the British North America Act, the federal government obtains full legislative powers. If it is interpreted as an activity which falls under exclusive provincial jurisdiction in the British North America Act, the federal government cannot legislate, but it can spend money on it.

Judicial interpretation of the key sections of the British North America Act of 1867 favored the evolution of Canadian federalism toward centralization from 1867 to 1896 (approximately) and from 1930 to 1970 (approximately). Very few questions of judicial interpretation remain unsettled and the accumulated judicial interpretation of the division of powers described in the British North America Act is now more significant than the Act itself. Parti Québécois leaders cannot accept the actual present-day division of powers arising from the interpretation of the British North America Act.

Moreover, the Parti Québécois leaders consider that the federal government is torn between two or more conflicting regional interests almost every time it faces a policy problem in the economic sector. It has to satisfy Alberta oil interests, Montreal refineries, the southern Ontario chemical industry, the automobile industry, and the average Canadian consumer. It has to balance the St. Lawrence harbor interests against the Great Lakes maritime interests and the Atlantic port interests. In the view of several Parti Québécois leaders, the prevailing interests win their point, and Quebec interests, if in conflict, register a loss.

According to the Parti Québécois program, Quebec political sovereignty would offer a variety of economic benefits to French-speaking Quebecers. Decisions which concern Quebec, instead of being made in Ottawa, would henceforth be made in Quebec by Quebecers and in a Quebec perspective. Savings would be made in taxation services, by a reorganization under one single Quebec authority of the Quebec Revenue Department and the Quebec branches of the federal Revenue Department. Corporate income tax, henceforth fully controlled by Quebec, would be used to promote Quebec industry and foster Quebec economic development. Individual income tax rates, also fully controlled by Quebec, would be modified so as to achieve greater justice and equity, being integrated with a guaranteed minimum income plan.

Excise taxes and production sales taxes, which are now the basic federal indirect taxes, would be integrated with the existing Quebec retail sales tax under a plan similar to the value-added tax common in Europe, with continued exemptions for food, pharmaceuticals, housing, and other essentials, and with higher rates for luxury products. Quebec economic development would benefit from greater co-ordination in the public sector, because one single government, Quebec, would be in charge of the whole sector, with a central planning board. In the fields of agriculture, forests, fisheries, mines and other resources, the Quebec government would be able to achieve greater productivity, a larger degree of industrial processing of primary products, better access to foreign markets, and so on, because it would have authority over the whole sector and because Quebec interests would be its primary objective.

The changes advocated by the Parti Québécois in the area of transport are a good example of its plans:

A Parti Québécois government pledges:
... to reorganize the transport field
a) by merging the railway systems in Quebec into a single system operated by a corporation that would be majority publicly-owned;
b) by unifying the domestic airlines and extending them to serve foreign destinations, as a single system also operated by a corporation that would be majority publicly-owned;
c) by administering navigation within Quebec's territorial limits, by favoring the creation of a merchant fleet through a realignment of companies and by maintaining the year-round navigability of the St. Lawrence River.[12]

The Socio-Cultural Aspect

In the social sector, the Parti Québécois believes that, because Quebec society is limited by the constraints of Canadian federalism, it cannot define priorities for its own social development. The federal institutional arrangement in Canada deprives Quebecers of the means required for public choices reflecting the characteristics of Quebec and enabling Quebec society to develop itself according to its own particular priorities. A politically sovereign Quebec would be able to offer better social services to its population, and it could do so at a lower cost than today, by eliminating fraud, administrative delay and program deficiencies, which now result from lack of co-ordination and excessive rivalry between federal and Quebec civil servants.

The elimination of Quebec-Ottawa rivalry is seen as a powerful argument by Parti Québécois propagandists. In the 1975 program, this paragraph follows a statement of health policy objectives:

The cost of drugs here is the highest in the world and allows the pharmaceutical industry to exploit commercially such a vital sector, with the tacit complicity of the federal government which contents itself with band-aids. ... Here as elsewhere, we will have to get rid of federal-provincial political struggles to widen the application of the health insurance program, to put an end to the exploitation of citizens in the area of drugs and to authorize an exceptional effort to improve the health of the population, notably through prevention and research.[13]

The section of the 1975 program devoted to work conditions states that "when it is relieved of the endless federal-provincial wrangling in the employment sector, Quebec will be in a position to guarantee genuine job security . . . ." As we have seen, the work situation differs somewhat from that in Ontario, as a result of greater territorial dispersal of the population, lower participation rate in the labor force, higher unemployment rates, crisis conditions in several manufacturing sub-sectors, and so on. Undoubtedly, the Parti Québécois has substantial arguments in calling for Quebec political sovereignty in these matters.

Another sector in which it holds a strong position is urban affairs. Urban planning and housing are unquestionably local matters. Nevertheless it is an area where the federal government has set a firm foot. According to the Parti Québécois, housing and urban planning constitute another area where federal policies and Quebec policies have always been different, if not contradictory.[14]

Quebec's housing situation is unique in that the percentage of families renting their housing is higher in Montreal (especially among French-speaking Montrealers) than anywhere else in Canada: overall, 53 per cent of Quebec dwellings are rented, while in no other province does the proportion of rented dwellings exceed 29 per cent.

The Parti Québécois position on the media is also probably supported by a large proportion of Quebec voters. In a politically sovereign Quebec, French would be the language of the publicly-owned radio and television networks, and the number of privately-owned English-language radio and television stations would be proportional to the English-speaking population of Quebec.[15] Privately-owned radio and television stations, in a sovereign Quebec governed by Parti Québécois leaders, could not be under non-resident control. Morever, co-operatives and community associations would obtain greater access to cable-television programming. In general, the Parti Québécois position is that Quebec should have the power to safeguard freedom of speech and opinion and to satisfy the desire of the Quebec people for means of cultural expression. Quebec political sovereignty and Parti Québécois policies would put Quebecers in control of the media and would curb the tendency toward private monopoly in the mass media.

Is Quebec Political Sovereignty a Solution that Canada Could Accept?

The arguments put forward in favor of Quebec political sovereignty by Parti Québécois leaders can be summarized under three main headings:

1) Quebec is different and most Canadian federal policies do not suit Quebec interests;

2) Federalism, as it is operating in Canada, is costly and inefficient;

3) The survival of a French-speaking society in North America cannot be guaranteed unless Quebec becomes a sovereign state.

These arguments are used in the Quebec constitutional debate along with the data which have been quoted above. Each argument and each set of data could be challenged. One can dispute the points relating to Quebec's share of federal revenue and its share of federal expenditures, because perspectives differ widely.

One can show that there is no such thing as a "Quebec national interest", but a variety of conflicting interests within Quebec, some of these being satisfied with Canadian federal policies while others are not. One can assert that the federal government is highly efficient, or that it is more efficient than the Quebec government. One can maintain that the costs of federalism are outweighed by benefits accruing from federalism. One can state his faith in the survival of French Quebec within the Canadian federation. There is indeed cause for dispute in the arguments used by Parti Québécois leaders, and the opposing contentions could be well documented. (The Quebec Liberal party thesis will be described at length in chapter 5.)

One can discard demographic projections, opinion surveys, or economic statistics on the grounds that the whole debate deals with sentiments, feelings, perceptions, moral values, and the like. Many of those who take part in the Quebec constitutional debate do not want to be confused with facts or figures. Moreover, they make a mountain out of the mole hill seen in their neighborhood: the facts and figures that count are personal experiences.

Both in Quebec and elsewhere, there have been many reactions to the election of the Parti Québécois. These reactions have ranged from desperation to incredulity, from excessive concern to the utmost indifference, even among Canadian political scientists and members of the Canadian Parliament. But outside Quebec, if one can judge by editorials and letters to the editor in the newspapers, by comments on radio hotlines, and by the statements of political leaders, those who have shown the greatest concern over the election are also those who seem the most worried by the prospect of Quebec's accession to political sovereignty. These same people are also those who are most inclined to want to crush "these separatists who want to break up Canada". Indeed, the Prime Minister of Canada, Pierre Trudeau, has been quoted as saying: "Quebec separatists have the choice between separation and association, but they can't have both."[16]

Others want to appease French Canadians. The leader of the Opposition, Joe Clark, told a Quebec audience on March 23, 1977, that he was willing to concede a lot more powers to the provinces in such areas as industrial development, culture, communications, immigration, urban affairs and mineral resources.[17] The day before, Claude Forget, who was Quebec's Minister of Social Affairs in the Bourassa government, had said that Ottawa should leave social affairs to the provinces.[18]

Many Canadians believe Quebec secession would be disastrous for the rest of Canada. A Gallup poll published March 23, 1977, revealed that 46 per cent of the Canadian sample thought that it would be very serious, 27 per cent quite serious, and 22 per cent not very serious.

But, according to another Gallup poll, published in the weekly *The Canadian* on April 9, 1977, 54.2 per cent of the English-speaking respondents said "no" to the following question: "Should the government of Canada negotiate special political and economic agreements with Quebec to try to prevent separation?" Among the French-speaking respondents, 66.9 per cent said "yes".

5

The Federalist Solution

Many members of the Quebec Liberal party, as well as many English-speaking Canadians outside Quebec, believe that if Quebec were to become a sovereign, separate country it would be dropping the substance for the shadow.

According to this point of view, the survival of the French language and of a French-speaking Quebec society can only be guaranteed by economic prosperity, and economic prosperity cannot be achieved in a separate Quebec. Consequently, in order to assure the survival of a French-speaking society in North America, Quebec must remain a province in the Canadian federation, albeit a province with more powers than before and, if necessary, more powers than other provinces.

This line of reasoning is a rebuttal of the Parti Québécois' argument that the survival of a French-speaking society in North America cannot be guaranteed unless Quebec becomes a sovereign state. This viewpoint is usually voiced in conjunction with other rebuttals of Parti Québécois arguments. According to many Quebec Liberals, Quebec is not significantly different from the rest of Canada, and if French Quebecers participated actively in the federal government, they would obtain federal policies suited to Quebec interests. In any case, add Quebec Liberals, federalism is less costly and more efficient than the "balkanization" proposed by the Parti Québécois.

Cultural Survival and Economic Prosperity

The leading postulate in the chain of anti-separatist reasoning is that cultural survival depends on economic prosperity. To support this idea, the drain of the French Quebec population between 1870 and 1930 is

127

usually cited. During this 60-year period, economic hardship in rural Quebec led several hundred thousand French Canadians to exile themselves to the United States. Is there anything worse than emigration to endanger the survival of a society?

The best-known case of language disappearance following an economic depression is provided by the Gaelic-speaking community of Ireland, which was destroyed by famine and migration during the second half of the nineteenth century. In 1850, Gaelic was spoken by half the population of Ireland. By 1900, it had become the language of a small minority. Examples such as these are numerous enough in America as well: Indian tribes have disappeared altogether after being reduced to poverty by Spanish conquerors or northern European settlers.

An economic disaster in Quebec, in the view of some Liberals, could be fatal to Quebec's French-speaking society. But the survival of a language and the culture associated with it does not depend solely on economic prosperity. It depends on a variety of other conditions as well: numbers, levels of education, cultural productivity, control of the media, exchanges, political factors. Quebec Liberals say that Quebec has or can easily obtain control over immigration and demographic policies (to maintain the "numbers"), over education, over cultural policies, over the media. And they are afraid of the economic disaster which, in their view, Quebec's political sovereignty would constitute.

Economic Consequences of Political Independence

According to the chain of reasoning developed by many Quebec Liberals, Quebec's accession to political independence would spell economic disaster, resulting from the loss of markets in Ontario and western Canada, a severe capital drain, the emigration of Quebec's economic elite, the loss of equalization payments, the loss of oil subsidies, and the budgetary deficits necessitated by the reorganization of the government and the moving of thousands of civil servants from Ottawa to Quebec.

In the view of leading Quebec Liberals, Quebec's accession to sovereignty would result in the loss of the Ontario and western markets now available to Quebec manufactured products protected by Canadian tariffs. These Quebec Liberals think that Quebec will never be able to negotiate "sovereignty and association", because English-speaking Canadians will jump at the opportunity to abolish the common tariffs which, at present, protect Quebec manufactured products. These protected Quebec products cost more than similar products manufactured in Taiwan, Hong Kong, Korea, Japan, Italy or Spain, but they still retain a share of the Canadian market because competing imported products are subject to tariffs and import quotas. If Quebec products lost their tariff protection in the rest of Canada, they would lose between 10 and 50 per cent of their market, depending on the product. These goods are already seriously endangered by foreign competition and vulnerable to tariff reductions and increased import quotas. The loss of the Ontario and western markets is bound to occur eventually, but it will constitute a serious setback if it occurs suddenly. If Quebec becomes independent, and the rest of Canada does not agree to a common market, this sudden setback would account for a decline in the Quebec Gross National Product of two to six per cent.

If Quebec sovereignty were achieved without a Quebec-Canada economic association, the Quebec textile, clothing, leather and electronics industries, to name a few, would be compelled to reorganize. The economic break-up of Canada would be felt mainly by the same industries which are already threatened by the possibility of Canadian tariff reductions and by foreign competition.

Quebec's accession to political sovereignty, with or without a Quebec-Canada economic association, would probably involve some capital drain. Some Liberals believe that this capital drain would be severe. Others say that most of the expected capital flight has occurred already. In any case, it is to be expected that a number of individuals who feel particularly insecure or who strongly disagree with the idea of a sovereign Quebec will as a first reaction stash their money abroad and, as a second reaction, exile themselves to Florida, California, Mexico or the Bahamas. These reactions to Quebec's accession to sovereignty could lead to some enterprises winding up, and some employees finding themselves without jobs.

More serious would be the emigration of Quebec economic elite: managers, accountants, engineers, entrepreneurs, chemists, and so on. This would probably occur among English-speaking Quebecers more than French-speaking Quebecers, but, no doubt, many French-speaking doctors, engineers and managers would be tempted to leave Quebec in fear of the future. If the person who leaves is not replaced, and if whole services move out of Quebec, then the loss can be felt by many people: secretaries and technicians can find themselves unemployed, office space and dwellings can be unoccupied for long periods, construction projects can lag. As a matter of fact, the brain drain has already started. As an example, according to calculations by Statistics Canada, between 1969 and 1973 several hundred thousand Quebecers left Quebec to go elsewhere, and the *net* emigration was 90,700. The greatest emigration occurred in the troubled years of 1970 and 1971, when 64,900 people left Quebec. In 1974 and 1975 more people came to Quebec than left: during these two years, there was a net immigration of 18,300 people. Since November 15, 1976, according to real-estate agents, the number of those leaving has been larger than the number of arrivals.

The threat of independence has been sufficient for many corporations to move personnel out of Quebec. In December 1976 the Royal Bank of Canada announced its decision to move some 100 people in its money market, investment and corporate marketing divisions from Montreal to Toronto. The Bank of Montreal moved about 25 people in its marketing department from Montreal to Toronto. Such moves have been a common occurrence in Montreal since the mid-1960s, when "separatism" began to gain momentum. These moves were particularly frequent in 1969 and 1970, at a time when uncertainty reached a high level, and they appear to be occurring at an even higher rate since the 1976 election. In any case, such moves always echo loudly in the news media. The effects of the flight from Quebec cannot be measured with certainty. Nevertheless they are significant and have been felt for a dozen years now.

Another aspect of the economic disaster predicted by some Quebec Liberals is the loss of equalization payments, oil subsidies, and other benefits accruing from "profitable federalism". As we have seen in recent years federal payments, expenditures and transfers to Quebec institutions and inhabitants have exceeded the amount of federal revenues collected in Quebec. While the statement of federal revenue and expenditure in Quebec cannot be considered a very serious argument either for or against Quebec sovereignty, it cannot be denied that, in the short run, the "reorganization of the public sector" following Quebec's accession to independence would be felt seriously.

One of the costs of Quebec's accession to sovereignty would involve moving public servants and their families from Ottawa to a location in Quebec. The Parti Québécois has pledged that no civil servant will lose his job or have his salary reduced following Quebec's accession to sovereignty. The cost of moving several thousand public servants and their families, households and offices from Ottawa to a location in

Quebec, and the low productivity that such a reorganization would involve for a period of several months can be estimated at $30,000 per public servant. If 15,000 public servants have to move—and the costs would be borne by the taxpayers—the price tag is a little over half a billion dollars. There can be no doubt that in the short run, for two or three years, Quebec's accession to sovereignty could cause major transition costs; according to Quebec Liberals, these would amount to "economic disaster".

Cultural Survival and the Canadian Federation

Quebec Liberals would rather play it safe. They are aware of the benefits which accrue from the maintenance of Quebec's federal links with the rest of Canada, and they are afraid of the economic consequences of Quebec's accession to sovereignty. To play it safe is to opt for the maintenance of federalism.

Actually, Quebec Liberals put the emphasis on economic development, not on "survival of a French-speaking Quebec society". In 1970, Robert Bourassa wrote: "Our great priority, first and foremost, has to be economic development. We must, by all the means at the disposal of the state, get our economy moving again. Without economic prosperity, we will never be able to attain the cultural and social objectives that we are all seeking."[19]

The survival of a French-speaking Quebec society depends on economic prosperity, and economic prosperity depends on Quebec's staying in the Canadian federation. On October 19, 1969, Bourassa was already saying: "The federal formula is without doubt the form of government which will assure Quebecers of the highest level of well-being, of their cultural development, of their active presence in the community of peoples and particularly of French-speaking peoples."[20]

From 1970 to 1973, as Premier of Quebec and leader of the Quebec Liberal party, Robert Bourassa undertook two major rounds of negotiations with the federal government. His first objective was to obtain a larger share of federal expenditures for Quebec, and he met with success, gaining significant increases in the area of equalization payments and regional economic development. The second objective was related to constitutional review: Quebec called for greater powers in the sectors of immigration, health, manpower, urban affairs, culture, education and youth. Unable to gain what it had requested, the Bourassa government vetoed the 1971 constitutional amendment formula, the Victoria Charter.

These constitutional objectives were reiterated in the Quebec Liberal party platform of 1973.[21] They were repeated anew in 1974 by the eighteenth convention of the party and again in 1976 by the nineteenth convention.

The 1976 convention recommended that the Quebec government approve a new federal-provincial division of legislative powers when and only when three fundamental guarantees had been included in the constitution: (a) provincial priority in the areas of communications and immigration; (b) the enlargement of provincial taxation powers and the restriction of federal spending powers; and (c) veto power over any proposed constitutional amendment for provinces with 20 per cent or more of the Canadian population. This position, adopted on April 25, 1976, constitutes the latest stand of the Quebec Liberal party on the "federal question". Resolutions at Liberal party conventions have rarely concerned the division of powers in Canada. Before 1960 the emphasis was put on autonomy, and a resolution on this subject was adopted at each convention. The platform of 1956 included the following text:

> The question of autonomy is not limited to taxes. It implies the right and the duty of each province to have and to implement a precise policy in all the areas allotted to it by the Canadian constitution: natural resources, education, agriculture, labor relations, health and welfare, etc.
>
> The absence of constructive and progressive provincial policies in these domains puts provincial autonomy in grave danger. The Liberal party has, on each of these points, a precise policy which is set out in this program and which will contribute to assuring the autonomy of Quebec on all fronts: economic, educational, social, etc.

During the 1960s, the emphasis shifted to specific questions, mostly related to the social affairs sector. The Quebec government succeeded in obtaining from Ottawa the power to "opt out" of joint federal-provincial programs in the sector of social affairs which, if exercised, meant gaining control over their operations and a fiscal compensation. When negotiations came to a standstill on the question of family allowances in 1966, the Quebec Liberals included the following sentence in their program: "As a means to allow the orderly implementation in Quebec of a social policy centred on the family and based on real needs, the government of Quebec will insist on the transfer from the federal government of family allowances."

In 1970, attention was focussed on three points: tax sharing between the federal and provincial governments, provincial control over radio and television, and immigration. On the taxation question, the 1970 Liberal program stated that a Liberal government would negotiate with Ottawa an increase in equalization and similar payments which would benefit Quebec. In addition, it would negotiate Quebec's participation in the policy-making process concerning tariffs on Quebec's manufactured products. In the communications sector, the 1970 platform stated that a Liberal government would negotiate with Ottawa Quebec's participation in policy-making related to radio and television. Finally, in the immigration sector, the 1970 platform called for federal-provincial co-operation in order to satisfy Quebec's objectives.

On the whole, the Quebec Liberals hold that Canada needs a flexible form of federalism, and that Quebec needs "cultural sovereignty" and "fiscal decentralization".

The underlying position is that Quebec is not really different from the remainder of Canada, except from the viewpoint of language and culture. Consequently, Quebec does not need special status in non-cultural areas. The extent of the cultural sector remains to be defined. However, as a minimum, it covers radio and television, education, arts and humanities, and most social programs, including immigration. The meaning of the slogan "cultural sovereignty" is that the Quebec government should have the last word in policy-making on the various questions pertaining to culture.

In another area, the Quebec Liberals consider that the Quebec government should raise the revenue it needs to match its expenditures. There should be a greater fiscal decentralization in Canada, an "economic federalism".

Benefits of Federalism

The Quebec Liberals have talked a lot about "profitable federalism". In using this term, they are saying two things. The first point is that one of the functions of the central government is to "equalize" public revenues among the different regions of the country. Quebec, with a 10 to 15 per cent lag behind the Canadian average per capita income, has benefited (or will benefit) from remaining a province within the Canadian federation. The second point is that a federation enables its member states to save a lot of money by sharing public services which would have to be duplicated if the federation did not exist. If Quebec were a separate country, it would have to maintain embassies abroad, a central bank, full-fledged statistical services, armed forces, and so on. The per capita costs of these services would be higher than their per capita cost in present-day Canada, because they cannot be one-fifth services. A Bank of Quebec would be at least one third the size of the present-day Bank of Canada. Federalism is profitable because it means savings on services which need not be duplicated and which are not local or regional by nature.

These are the Liberals' chief counter-arguments to the Parti Québécois's position in favor of sovereignty. They add that the federal setup can and will be improved, and that their policy is directed precisely toward avoiding costly duplication and making federalism profitable. In the view of Quebec Liberal party leaders, the federal system which links together the various regions of Canada has many other advantages, related to foreign affairs and international trade as well as to domestic questions. The "balkanization" of Canada would constitute a loss for the whole country.

In the area of defence, the theoretical advantages of federalism are considerable. The Canadian armed forces are considerably more efficient than would be two separate, barely co-ordinated Canadian and Quebec military organizations. Indeed, to achieve the degree of efficiency and defensive capability maintained by the Canadian armed forces today the total budget required for two separate military organizations would be, as a rough estimate, 25 per cent higher. But, of course, a separate Quebec could try to operate without rescue patrols, without coast guards, without northern outposts, without emergency services, without radars, without any participation in the United Nations peacekeeping operations!

Similar arguments are advanced concerning the advantages of federalism in foreign affairs and international trade. Quebec Liberals and most English-speaking Canadians consider that great advantages accrue from the maintenance of one common department of external affairs, one common network of trade agencies and immigration offices, one common foreign aid agency, and so forth. If the Canadian territory were balkanized, and if each separate region were to maintain embassies, consulates, trade offices, immigration offices, and so on, the total costs to taxpayers would be a lot higher than today.

Quebec Liberals add that, in spite of acknowledged difficulties, Quebec benefits from the weight carried by Canada in the world. French-speaking Canadians travelling abroad have their embassy. Quebec enterprises which want to export can benefit from the extensive network of Canadian trade agencies. Canada projects a favorable image in every country of the world and this is to the advantage of French-speaking Quebecers. Indeed, indirect benefits such as these, according to some Quebec Liberals, outweigh the inadequacies of Canadian foreign policy that are so often cited by the Parti Québécois.

Quebec Liberals also stress the advantages accruing from the maintenance of a consumer market of 22 million people in Canada. If Canadian territory were divided into two or more separate markets, Quebec would find itself confined to its own market of six million. In addition, there are the benefits of standardization: monetary standardization, fiscal standardization, manufacturing standardization, weights and measures, postal and telephone services, and so forth. Another theoretical benefit of federalism, as compared with "balkanization", is found in the launching of vast long-term projects in the common interest: building transcontinental railways, laying transcontinental pipelines, developing networks of airports, digging canals and seaways. Robert Bourassa, who was a friend of René Lévesque's and worked closely with him before Lévesque left the Liberal party in 1967, was well aware of the objections of Parti Québécois members to Liberal arguments in favor of federalism. But he used to say that the objections raised always referred to the past, and often the facts and figures quoted referred to the nineteenth century. The statistics on railways and canals, for instance, concerned federal projects which were practically completed by 1900. Moreover, although only small portions of the railway and canal networks are located in Quebec, there is no question that they helped make Montreal the commercial, financial and industrial centre of Canada, at least up to the 1960s. During his six-year term as Quebec Premier, Bourassa kept saying that it was time to forget about the past and start looking to the future.

It might be true that, all in all, federalism has not been as beneficial to French-speaking Quebecers as it could have been but, say the Liberals, the situation has changed. Quebec has become a developed, urbanized society. Quebecers have acquired the necessary technical know-how and they can now play their part in the Canadian adventure. The theoretical advantages of federalism can henceforth be fully felt by French-speaking Quebecers. Quebec already benefits from the twenty-year-old equalization program, from the ten-year-old regional economic expansion program, from the five-year-old Quebec-Ottawa agreement in the social sector, from the three-year-old oil subsidy. By gaining full control over cultural matters, Quebec could have the best of two worlds: the advantages of cultural sovereignty and the benefits of economic federalism. Is that not far simpler and easier than "sovereignty-association"? According to Quebec Liberals, federalism offers all the benefits and none of the risks.

6

Third Options

Between the Parti Québécois's "sovereignty-association" proposal and the Quebec Liberal party's "profitable federalism", there is ample ground for third options.

The Union Nationale, led by Rodrigue Biron, comes close to what could be termed a third option, midway between the Parti Québécois's constitutional proposals and the Quebec Liberal party's "flexible federalism". The smaller political parties do not have elaborate constitutional programs: some of them stand for Canadian federalism as it is today, while others call for a socialist Canada and reject the constitutional question altogether.

The Constitutional Stand of the Union Nationale

The Union Nationale has a long tradition as a defender of provincial autonomy and decentralization. Between 1936 and 1959, under the leadership of Maurice Duplessis, the party systematically opposed federal centralization, even refusing federal grants and denying Quebec the benefits offered by Ottawa to the provinces surrendering to its fiscal proposals. Between 1966 and 1968, under the leadership of Daniel Johnson, the Union Nationale posed an ultimatum to Ottawa: equality or independence. Premier Johnson stood firmly in favor of an arrangement midway between traditional Canadian federalism and Quebec independence, but he was talking seriously when he said that Quebec would rather declare its independence unilaterally than agree to the type of federalism which was being perpetuated in Canada. Gabriel Loubier, who led the Union Nationale from 1971 to 1974, defined Canada as the union of two nations. This thesis of two nations led to constitutional proposals similar to those which Daniel Johnson had presented to the federal government as Premier between 1966 and 1968.

Other leaders of the Union Nationale (Premier Paul Sauvé, 1959; Premier Antonio Barette, 1960; Premier Jean-Jacques Bertrand, 1968 to 1970; and Maurice Bellemare, 1974 to 1976) did not modify its fundamental constitutional stand. And when he became leader of the Union Nationale in May 1976, Rodrigue Biron inherited the autonomist thesis of his party. This autonomist thesis was confirmed by the party convention held during the first week of October 1976, 15 days before the launching of the election campaign which led to the Union Nationale's gaining 11 seats in the National Assembly.

The Union Nationale stands for a highly decentralized form of federalism. This proposed new federalism would give the "reserve power" to the provinces and would confirm the full and complete sovereignty of the provincial governments over education, health, social security, communications, cultural affairs, and the matters which already fall under provincial jurisdiction according to existing judicial interpretation of the British North America Act of 1867.

Moreover, under the new federalism defined by Union Nationale literature, the provincial governments would have *exclusive* responsibility over policy-making and administration, within provincial territory, in matters related to immigration, regional economic development, housing and urban planning and land management. In addition, provincial governments would have the power to negotiate, sign and administer international agreements in the various sectors falling under their jurisdiction. Finally, the powers of the federal government would be drastically curbed, not only through the transfers implied in the enlargement of exclusive provincial jurisdictions, but also through severe restrictions put on the federal government's spending power and taxation capabilities. And, in order to avoid the pitfalls of centralizing judicial interpretation, the new federalism of the Union Nationale would be safeguarded by a constitutional court on which would sit judges chosen and appointed by the provincial governments.

During the 1976 election campaign, Union Nationale spokesmen were careful not to publicize their program and they simply told their audiences that they stood "four-square" for Quebec's remaining in Canada, that they favored a renewed federalism, and that they were the federalist alternative to the Liberals. On October 29, 1976, Premier Robert Bourassa told English-speaking Liberal supporters on Ile Perrot near Montreal that the Union Nationale was "not a federalist party". He said the Union Nationale "proposes associate-state status for Quebec in relation to the rest of Canada. If you look at their program you'll see that they don't really believe in the federal system." He added that the Quebec Liberal party "is the only federalist party".[22] Bourassa's opinion was echoed by candidate Bryce Mackasey, former federal minister, campaigning in Notre-Dame-de-Grâce riding in the English-speaking west end of Montreal. Rodrigue Biron reacted by saying that he was a federalist and that he stood for a regenerated federalism.

Nevertheless, a study of the Union Nationale's 1976 program, as well as its programs of 1973 and 1966, leads to the following conclusion: the Union Nationale stands for a constitutional solution midway between sovereignty-association and traditional federalism. One can remember Union Nationale Premier Daniel Johnson declaring to other premiers at a meeting in Ottawa, September 14 and 15, 1966:

> In preparation for the new constitution, it is also important that we proceed without delay with a rearrangement of revenues and functions between the federal and Quebec governments. By virtue of this rearrangement, the Quebec government would gradually become solely responsible within its territory for all public expenditures relating to education in all its forms, old-age security, family allowances, manpower placement and training, regional development and especially aid to municipalities, research, fine arts, culture and, in general, all other services of a socio-cultural nature which are our responsibility by virtue of the present constitution....
>
> Quebec believes that the best way to rearrange revenues between itself and the federal government is to reserve to Quebec the full use of 100 per cent of the sources of fiscal revenue to which it has a right constitutionally, that is personal and corporate income taxes and succession duties.[23]

Johnson's proposals were consonant with the text of the British North America Act of 1867. They were not "separatist". Nevertheless, they were labelled "crypto-separatist" and the Union Nationale was said to be supporting a "two-nation thesis". The reactions to the Union Nationale's constitutional proposals of 1976 are similar to those which met Premier Daniel Johnson's proposals ten years before. But those reactions did not stop the federal government from introducing changes in its policies which satisfied several of Johnson's demands. Compromises were negotiated. Quebec eventually obtained half the personal income tax levied in Quebec and it gained control over several social programs. Quebec got a separate pension plan, participation in family allowances, control of its health programs and so on.

The Parti National Populaire and the Ralliement Créditiste

Apart from the Union Nationale, which won 18 per cent of the votes cast and 11 of the 110 seats in the Quebec National Assembly in November 1976, each of two other small parties succeeded in having one candidate elected. The Ralliement Créditiste polled four per cent of the vote and its leader, Camil Samson, was elected in the constituency of Rouyn-Noranda in northwestern Quebec. The Parti National Populaire, created by dissident former Liberal minister Jérôme Choquette and a former Créditiste, Fabien Roy, less than a year before the election, received one per cent of the total vote and saw Roy elected in the constituency of Beauce-Sud, in the southeastern part of the province. These two smaller parties profess to support federalism and their leaders have stated repeatedly that they want Quebec to stay within Canada.

Delegates to the first convention of the Parti National Populaire, held a few days after the opening of the 1976 election campaign, opted for a restoration of the power of the provinces but did not adopt any specific constitutional proposal. They focussed their attention on matters falling in well-established provincial jurisdiction. Only four proposals made reference to the federal government or to federal programs or policies. One of these concerned immigration and said that "immigration policy had to be consonant with Quebec language policy". Another was related to family allowances and called for a graduated scale geared to fostering increased birthrates. A third one supported predominant jurisdiction for the Quebec government in all matters related to the manufacturing sector. The last of these proposals was a rebuttal to federal policies aimed at Quebec credit unions and co-operatives. Perhaps as a result of these stands, the party's election pamphlet made no mention of the word "federalism".

The leader of the Parti National Populaire, Jérôme Choquette, made several pleas in support of a reinforced Canadian federalism. He said that "the basis of the Canadian union should not be put in question". On October 14, 1976, his views were expressed in these words:

> The Canadian union is the guarantee of Quebec's prosperity. Separation will bring about extreme economic hardship resulting principally from lack of investment and loss of markets. Canada will retaliate by erecting tariff walls to the detriment of Quebec. Federalism is not only a paying proposition, it is indispensable. Quitting Canada, Quebec will become a member of the poor nations' club of this earth.... We refuse to let Quebec become an obscure Balkan state lost in Anglo-Saxon North America.

In contrast to their Parti National Populaire opponents, Ralliement Créditiste candidates entered the 1976 election campaign with a well-established platform. In constitutional matters, the Ralliement Créditiste platform was squarely "anti-separatist". But in spite of its federalist stand, the Ralliement Créditiste supported a kind of special status for Quebec. It was in favor of Quebec's using all available powers over trade and immigration. It supported the idea that the Quebec government should take full advantage of section 92, paragraph 2, of the British North America Act, which gives provincial legislatures the power to levy revenues for provincial purposes by means of direct taxation. In the view of Créditiste spokesmen, the federal government should be ejected from the income-tax field. The Ralliement Créditiste considered that "credit" should be controlled by provincial governments. Communications (the mass media) and territorial development were also said to belong to the provinces.

The 1976 election pamphlets of the Ralliement Créditiste were in the tradition of the constitutional stand taken by the leaders of the party in April 1971, when a fifteen-page text was signed by the then twelve Créditiste members of the Quebec National Assembly and the five members of the party executive committee. This constitutional manifesto was published in the May 1971 issue of the party monthly, *L'ordre nouveau*. It called for the abolition of the monarchy in Canada and of the whole British North America Act of 1867 (page 8 of the manifesto). It supported the right of each province to determine its own constitutional future. On the whole, these constitutional options were in line with statements set forth by the leaders of the movement since 1963, and they were thought to reflect the dominant opinion of the rank-and-file, however sketchy they might appear when compared with the Parti Québécois program.

The Left-Wing Parties

A dozen political parties have no parliamentary representation. Altogether, their candidates polled fewer than one per cent of the votes cast in the 1976 election. These very small parties constitute the left wing of the Quebec political spectrum. One, the Democratic Alliance, describes itself as a "progressive reform movement". Another poses as a "workers' movement". A third one calls itself the Quebec Workers' Party. And there is the traditional Quebec Communist Party. And the Groupe Marxiste Revolutionnaire (three candidates). And the League for Socialist Action (one candidate). And the North American Labour Party (one candidate). And the Parti Communiste du Québec (Marxiste-Léniniste), the Canadian Communist League (Marxist-Leninist), and the Maoist promoters of a future Canadian Proletarian Party (Marxist-Leninist), who publish *In Struggle* and *Proletarian Unity*.

Two of these parties favor federalism: this is the case with the Democratic Alliance led by Nick Auf der Maur (13 candidates, 17,444 votes, in 1976) and with the coalition formed by the Quebec New Democratic Party and a moderate Trotskyist organization known as the Regroupement des Militants Syndicaux, with the support of another Trotskyist organization called the Groupe Socialiste des Travailleurs du Québec. Among the 21 candidates of the coalition, three or four distinct constitutional stands could be identified. Some candidates were heard saying that they favored a complete overhaul of the Canadian constitution, while others stated a marked preference for the current arrangement. The 14 candidates of the Quebec Communist Party tried to stay away from the constitutional debate, and the 1,770 voters who supported them were apparently concerned with other problems.

All in all, even if they favored federalism, the leaders of these three small parties (which were the largest in the left wing) agreed with the right of Quebec to decide its own future and with the idea of amending the century-old division of power between the central Parliament and the provincial legislatures. Others among the small parties favored Quebec's accession to political sovereignty and supported the idea of a socialist Quebec. This was the case with the Quebec Workers' Party (12 candidates, 1,248 votes), the League for Socialist Action (one candidate, 88 votes), and the Groupe Marxiste Révolutionnaire (three candidates, 122 votes). The remaining groups altogether accounted for only three candidates and 207 votes and their dominant characteristic was concern with theory, not with Quebec realities.

Is There a Third Option?

If there is a third option, it does not come from any of the left-wing parties. The socialist parties cannot win a single constituency and they are too divided for an electoral union to be a serious possibility. Although united behind the objective of advancing the class struggle, their members fight against each other in labor unions and citizens committees. Nor is anything to be expected from the Ralliement Créditiste or the Parti National Populaire. Their constitutional stands need further explanation. In any case, constitutional problems are not the priority of these parties, which are more concerned with the social policies of the Quebec government.

The third option is found in the Union Nationale platform. It goes further in the way of provincial autonomy than the Quebec Liberals dare venture, but it remains a federalist option.

Is a third option representative of a large proportion of Quebec public option? As an answer one can quote opinion polls taken since 1970. The least that can be said is that any midway option gains more support than the "sovereignty" proposal, and more support than options which stand for no change. But opinions shift. As we know, Parti Québécois leaders anticipate a majority in support of Quebec independence by 1980 or 1982.

The third constitutional option proposed by the Union Nationale, even though it has the support of much of the population, cannot be considered by Union Nationale leaders as a road to electoral victory. The Union Nationale organization is made up of three main categories of party workers, only two of which support the constitutional stand of the party.

One category consists of English-speaking conservatives who would rather stand with the Quebec Liberal party on constitutional matters although they disapprove of the Liberals' economic and social policies. The second category approves of the Union Nationale's stand on constitutional matters but is closer to the Parti Québécois in economic matters and closer to the Quebec Liberal party in social matters; this category is made up of French-speaking Union Nationale supporters of the younger generation. The third category is made up of the older Union Nationale faithful: they approve of the nationalist stand of their party, favor economic policies directed toward small and medium-sized enterprises (like the younger generation and like the dominant wing of the Parti Québécois) and are opposed to the Parti Québécois's pro-labor stand and the Quebec Liberal party's social policies, notably in education and welfare.

The Union Nationale is a coalition of groups, which have one thing in common: they all stand in favor of private initiative and small and medium-sized enterprises, and are all dissatisfied with the political action of labor unions in Quebec. It would be hard to enlarge this coalition because what it stands for can satisfy sympathizers of neither the Parti Québécois nor the Liberal party.

In an election, moreover, the choices made by voters reflect a variety of motivations and influences. As an example, in the 1976 election, only seven per cent of the voters surveyed by sociologists Maurice Pinard and Richard Hamilton put "independence" as the most important issue of the campaign, while eight per cent put it as the second most important issue. Another two per cent put "constitution" first, and seven per cent held it as the second most important issue. High above these issues, according to the survey data, the voters ranked "the economy", "public morality", and "right to strike". The language question was seen as a more important issue than independence (and the other issues) by six per cent of the respondents. In other words, even in 1976, the constitutional stand of a party was not of overwhelming importance for its campaign strategy or for its electoral success. As a matter of fact, the Union Nationale tried to play down its constitutional option during the campaign. In its English-language advertising, the Union Nationale did not even mention its proposal for a new federalism, although it did it in its French-language advertising.

The electoral gains obtained by the Union Nationale were concentrated in two areas of the province. The first area was the English-speaking western part of Montreal and the English-speaking southern rural constituencies bordering the United States. The other area contained traditional Union Nationale strongholds: the rural and semi-rural constituencies located south of the St. Lawrence, between the Richelieu and Chaudière rivers. These areas are those where the ideas upheld by the Union Nationale are strongest.

Table 6—The Most Important Issues in the November 1976 Campaign

	Ranked first by	*Ranked second by*
The economy	41%	30%
The honesty of the government	29%	23%
The right to strike in the public sector	12%	18%
Independence	7%	8%
Bill 22 – and enrolment in English schools	6%	11%
Canadianization of the constitution	2%	7%
All issues equally important/no answer/ don't know	2%	3%
Number of answers	(1,095)	(1,091)

Source: A survey directed by sociologists Richard Hamilton and Maurice Pinard, in *Le Devoir, The Gazette* and The *Toronto Star*, November 10, 1976.

A Third Option and the Referendum

In a referendum, just as in an election, the choices made by the voters reflect a variety of motivations and perceptions, but instead of half a dozen options, the ballot offers only two: black or white, yes or no. Past experience, in countries such as France and Switzerland where referendums have been held recently, shows that the party in power normally has the support of its sympathizers and that smaller parties usually carry considerable weight.

Four of the five recent French referendums worked out to the advantage of the ruling Gaullist party. In September 1958, the Gaullists got 80 per cent of the voters to approve their proposed constitution. The referendums of January 1961 and April 1962, concerning the status of Algeria, were also won by the Gaullists and put an end to the Algerian independence conflict: the Gaullists got 75 per cent of the votes cast in the first referendum and 90 per cent in the second. The October 1962 referendum, providing for the election of the French president by direct universal popular suffrage for a seven-year term, was another Gaullist victory: in spite of the opposition of all the other parties, the Gaullists got 60 per cent of the popular vote. The only referendum which "failed" in modern France was the April 1969 referendum proposing a substantial governmental decentralization, labelled "regionalization". The idea was opposed by traditional elites, who benefited from the status quo, by the left-wing parties, who opposed anything that looked Gaullist, and by some people such as Valéry Giscard d'Estaing who normally supported de Gaulle. The result was 47 per cent for de Gaulle, 53 per cent against, and it forced the General's resignation.

A study of voting behavior and party strategies in referendums held in France, Switzerland and other countries provides useful ideas on the politics of constitutional referendums. The first point worth noting is that, just as in an election, the decision on how to vote in a referendum is the result of numerous influences, one of which, and not necessarily the strongest, is the precise wording of the question. Among the factors taken into account, one of the most important is related to "perspective": is the proposed text the result of a negotiation, or a compromise proposal aimed at a settlement, or a starting position in a renewed conflict? Does the proposed text focus on language, or on economic growth, or on representative and efficient government?

The alliance which is formed in support of the proposed text is another very important factor. Party strategy and the interests of various pressure groups usually determine the nature of such an alliance. Perhaps the most interesting questions concern the possible strategy of the Union Nationale. The third option which has been advanced by the Union Nationale cannot take it to power in an election, unless the party is able to gain support from some former Liberals, some former Parti Québécois sympathizers and some former Créditistes. But to achieve this, it must find interests that all these people share with Union Nationale supporters.

In 1973, Union Nationale leader Gabriel Loubier tried to stand for every option that seemed to have the support of a majority: a middle-of-the-road constitutional option, a moderately progressive social stand, and so on. He met with failure because the voters could not reconcile the conflicting elements in Loubier's platform as easily as he could. Those who were pleased with the social stand of the party were not satisfied with its tradition, while those who used to support the Union Nationale were not happy with its new social policy. Loubier and his candidates got 146,206 votes in the October 1973 election, a loss of more than 400,000 from the 564,544 the voters had given to the Union Nationale three years before.

In a referendum, the support given by the Union Nationale to one or the other option would largely depend on its future electoral strategy. If the potential clientele of the Union Nationale in a future election is to come from the ranks of the Quebec Liberal party, its interest would be in defeating the Liberals first in the referendum. In such an eventuality, Parti Québécois leaders could come up with a question that appeared to be a compromise between its own constitutional stand and the Union Nationale's constitutional option. The hope of displacing the Liberals as the official opposition—and eventually, the Parti Québécois as the majority party—would be decisive for the Union Nationale. A coalition of the Union Nationale and the Parti Québécois on the referendum question might appear a strange alliance, but it is not an impossible one.

If the potential clientele of the Union Nationale was thought to come from the ranks of the Parti Québécois, its strategy would be different. The Union Nationale leaders would then water down their constitutional option and side with the Quebec Liberals. A coalition of the Union Nationale and the Quebec Liberal party on the referendum question would constitute such a tough opposition that the Parti Québécois would have to muster for full-time service every one of its 120,000 members in order to gain the required majority. But then, if the Parti Québécois won, that would probably kill the hopes of the opposition leaders of ever gaining power in Quebec.

Any discussion of a third option for Quebec should take into account electoral trends registered in Quebec since the 1950s (as shown in table 7). It should be remembered that, even though the choices offered to voters in a referendum are restricted to yes-or-no or black-or-white alternatives, the influences at play remain numerous, conflicting, and powerful. The alignment of the political parties, finally, can be the most significant factor.

Table 7 – Distribution of Valid Ballots, as a Proportion of Voters on the Electoral Lists (not as a proportion of total valid ballots) and Distribution of Seats Among the Major Political Parties, Quebec Assembly, 1935–1976 (in percentages)

Election (year)	Voters on lists (number)	Valid ballots (number)	Number of seats	Liberal Party Votes	Liberal Party Seats	Union Nationale Votes	Union Nationale Seats	Parti Québécois Votes	Parti Québécois Seats	Other parties Votes	Other parties Seats
1935	726,551	536,361	90	37.0	53.3	36.0	46.7	—	—	0.8	0.0
1936	734,025	569,325	90	32.4	15.6	44.6	84.4	—	—	0.5	0.0
1939	753,310	563,297	86	40.5	81.4	29.3	17.4	—	—	4.9	1.2
1944	1,864,692	1,345,518	91	28.5	40.3	25.8	52.8	—	—	17.8	6.9
1948	2,036,576	1,513,825	92	28.5	8.7	37.9	89.1	—	—	7.9	2.2
1952	2,246,889	1,679,272	92	34.4	25.0	38.5	73.8	—	—	1.9	1.2
1956	2,393,350	1,845,729	93	34.3	21.5	40.1	77.4	—	—	3.5	1.1
1960	2,608,439	2,096,597	95	41.2	53.7	37.5	45.2	—	—	1.7	1.1
1962	2,721,933	2,136,966	95	44.3	64.1	33.0	32.6	—	—	1.2	3.3
1966	3,222,302	2,324,829	108	34.0	46.3	29.5	51.9	—	—	8.6	1.8
1970	3,478,891	2,872,970	108	37.5	66.6	16.2	15.5	19.0	6.5	9.8	11.4
1973	3,762,709	2,970,709	110	43.2	92.7	3.9	0.0	23.8	5.5	8.0	1.8
1976	4,025,118	3,361,963	110	28.2	25.5	15.2	10.0	34.6	62.7	2.8	1.8

If the alignment of political parties depended on nothing but the constitutional preferences of their most active members, chances are that the Quebec Liberal party would find itself isolated. As Robert Bourassa said repeatedly during the 1976 election campaign, the Quebec Liberal party is the only genuine federalist party in Quebec, and even at that it calls for Quebec control over immigration and culture, including the media.

The most politically active citizens in Quebec are much more nationalist in outlook than the whole of the population. This phenomenon is easily explained by the fact that the most active citizens come from the ranks of those who are better educated and better paid, who have more leisure or can afford more time, and who, generally, are leaders in their community. Now these citizens are precisely those who hold the strongest nationalist feelings and who are the most concerned about the future of their society. As a result, all political parties are run by people who favor greater constitutional changes than do the party's sympathizers. The active membership of the Union Nationale is definitely strongly nationalist and autonomist. But the most active members do not decide everything.

The Quebec electorate is crisscrossed by lines of cleavage which make it difficult for any party to gain a large majority in elections to the National Assembly. The Quebec Liberal party, in 1970 and 1973, was able to unite conflicting categories by focussing on the "independence question": it rallied the whole of the English-speaking electorate as well as many well-to-do, traditionalist French-speaking voters on its stand against separatism. At the same time, in 1970 and 1973, it got the votes of French-speaking voters who favored the Liberals' advocacy of large job creating government projects such as the James Bay hydro complex and the Montreal Olympic games, and who supported Liberal policies in the social sector.

In 1976, warnings against the separatist threat did not bring the Liberals the expected results, partly because the Parti Québécois soft-pedalled the issue and partly because many voters were not prepared to take the threat seriously a third time in a row. The great government projects had proved very costly while the number of jobs created was not that large. These projects had been an opportunity for pilfering public coffers, and suspicion of corruption in government had mounted to a very high level. Finally, the social policies of the Liberal government had been revealed as somewhat deceptive: language legislation had antagonized significant segments of the electorate, and the government's handling of labor disputes, especially in the public sector, had raised considerable opposition.

In Quebec today the electorate is divided on economic policies. It is divided on labor policies, it is divided on educational standards and education management, and it is divided on the constitutional formula. These cleavages are worsened by the division between French-speaking Quebecers and English-speaking Quebecers, and by the differences in interests and perspective between Montreal voters and the rest of the electorate.

There is a broad consensus in the French-speaking Quebec electorate, however, on the great objectives of national survival, economic development, and Quebec government supremacy, the last objective reflecting a desire to make Quebec the homeland of French-speaking Canadians. The Parti Québécois holds an advantage over its rivals from this point of view because it is the party which has taken the clearest stand in support of these three fundamental objectives, although they are also upheld, with lesser emphasis, by every other party. The Parti Québécois also holds another advantage in that it is unchallenged in Montreal's French-speaking constituencies, while it can gain many new votes outside Montreal by maintaining and advertising its economic platform, which favors the interests of the province's regions.

The compromise favored by some members of the Parti Québécois, full economic union between a federal Canada and a politically sovereign Quebec, could turn out to constitute the much-sought third option.* In any case, if a third option is to prevail in the next few years, it can only do so with the support of the Parti Québécois membership.

* Two members of the Parti Québécois parliamentary representation have been quoted on this point, Claude Morin, minister of intergovernmental affairs, and Gérald Godin, member for the district of Mercier.

Notes to Part II

1. New Democratic Party of Quebec, *Platform*, page 10, translation.
2. Claude Morin, *Le pouvoir québécois... en négociation* (Montreal: Les Editions de Boréal-Express, 1972), pages 64-66.
3. *Le programme, l'action politique, les statuts et règlements, edition 1975* (Montreal: Parti Québécois, 1975), page 5, translation.
4. Ibid.
5. *Le Supplément du Samedi, Le Journal de Montréal*, November 13, 1976.
6. *Le programme*, page 5, translation.
7. Ibid., page 18. The same text also appears in *Un gouvernement du Parti Québécois s'engage* (Montreal: Parti Québécois, 1973), page 72.
8. Rodrigue Tremblay, *Indépendance et marché commun Québec-Etats-Unis* (Montreal: Editions du Jour, 1970).
9. *Enough is Enough—The English and the '76 Election* (Montreal: Parti Québécois, 1976), page 8.
10. *Le coup du fédéralisme* (Montreal: Parti Québécois, 1973), page 7.
11. Ibid., page 11.
12. *Le programme*, page 13, translation.
13. Ibid., page 20.
14. Ibid., page 23.
15. Ibid., page 25.
16. See the *Financial Post*, April 30, 1977, pages 1, 4.
17. *Le Devoir*, March 24, 1977, page 1.
18. *Le Devoir*, March 23, 1977, page 2.

19. Robert Bourassa, *Bourassa Québec!* (Montreal: Les Editions de l'Homme, 1970), page 11, translation.

20. Ibid., page 26.

21. *Un nouveau programme d'action 1973* (Montreal: Parti Libéral du Québec, 1973), pages 75-77.

22. *The Gazette*, Montreal, October 30, 1976, page 40.

23. Reproduced in *Le gouvernement du Québec et la constitution* (Quebec: Office of Information and Publicity, 1968), pages 7-8, translation.

CONCLUSION

Prime Minister Pierre Elliott Trudeau insists that the Quebec nationalists will be unable to stand by their convictions when faced with the economic consequences of their nationalism. An opinion survey sponsored by the CBC French network a few days after the November 15, 1976 election tends to support the views of Prime Minister Trudeau. This survey was conducted by sociologists Maurice Pinard and Richard Hamilton, who used the same methods and the same sample as they had two weeks earlier when they were able to measure accurately the relative strength of the parties competing in the election. The survey showed that the new "fact" constituted by the election results coincided with a dramatic drop in support for the "independence option". The survey taken during the first week of November had shown that 18 per cent of the 1,097 respondents were in favor of Quebec's becoming an independent country, 58 per cent were against, and 24 per cent abstained on the question. Two weeks later, 11 per cent of the 1,088 respondents were in favor, 68 per cent were opposed, and 26 per cent were abstaining—a drop of seven percentage points in 15 days!

If it is true that Quebec nationalists will be unable to sustain their convictions in the face of the economic consequences of their nationalism, they might give a majority to the sovereignty-association formula in a public opinion poll and, in a referendum, defeat such an option. This possibility reassures many people who would otherwise be more concerned about the survey data which show that the long-term trend favors the sovereignty option. Yet in spite of occasional drops such as the one revealed by Pinard and Hamilton, the long-term trend is a one percentage point growth per year in the support given to the independence option in Quebec.

153

If it is true that Quebec nationalists are afraid of the economic consequences of their nationalism, it may be possible to negotiate even with a Quebec government pledged to achieve Quebec independence. A comparison of the "starting positions" held by Quebec premiers in federal-provincial conferences since 1945 with their "final stands" after months of frustrating negotiations makes it clear that, so far, Quebec nationalist leaders have always compromised. Many people expect the same of the Parti Québécois. They believe that the whole affair is nothing but a background for negotiation, and state peremptorily that Quebec will never separate.*

Politicians such as federal Finance Minister Jean Chrétien, on the other hand, argue that the very vocal, well-educated, "separatist" minority will never surrender to any compromise. People must learn to live with "separatism" but not to fear "separatism" or "separation", because "separation" will never happen. In the same line of thought, others argue that the presence of the English-speaking minority in Quebec is a guarantee that there will never be a majority behind the sovereignty-association formula. English-speaking Quebecers are thought to be solidly opposed to such a formula, and, totaling 20 per cent of the Quebec electorate, they are able to stop up to 65 per cent of the French-speaking Quebecers from having their say.

This may be reassuring for many Canadians, but will this English-speaking bloc ultimately be an obstacle to sovereignty-association? How many "federalist voters" will have already left Quebec by the time the referendum is held? How many bilingual English-speaking Quebecers will join the Parti Québécois forces? How many Quebec voters will find sovereignty less costly than an indefinite continuation of the uncertainty that has already caused so many problems?

If a satisfactory compromise is not reached in the near future, the long-term trend toward pro-independence sentiment is likely to be maintained. And if it is maintained, the disruptive trends will continue. Some commentators link Quebec economic problems to the action of the pro-independence movement.** In their view, "separa-

* Quotations to that effect are found every week in most newspapers. For easy reference, see the *Reader's Digest* article on the future of Canada in the October, 1977, issue of this widely read monthly.

** One example is provided by the April 1977 decision of Warnock Hersey International Ltd. to move the 16 employees of its head office out of Quebec. Its treasurer, C. G. Penney, told *The Montreal Star*:

tism" has done more harm to the Quebec economy than factors such as demography, geography and industrial structure. According to these commentators, "separatist agitation" in Quebec has scared away small and medium-sized investors as well as some larger manufacturing firms. They have preferred to invest their capital in safer places. This movement of investment capital out of Quebec, which was already occurring as a result of the general westward trend of North American economy, has been hastened by the separatist threat. Indeed, say some people, the costs of Quebec's future independence are already being paid every day.

Parti Québécois members reply by saying that this tax on the future will cease to apply when Quebec becomes independent. What Quebec pays now is the price of fear: fear of the future, fear of change. According to Parti Québécois members, this price is the cost of a lack of maturity on the part of too many voters; in a sense, these Parti Québécois members fully agree with Prime Minister Trudeau: if French-speaking Quebecers give in to their fears, they will be unable to hold to their nationalist convictions. As long as there is only "separatist agitation", the price of fear will continue to be paid. The Parti Québécois members want to convince Quebecers to overcome their fear and become "independent". Until now, they say, the federal arrangement has been detrimental to French-speaking Quebecers, and in the future it will be worse still—so let's change this and opt for a better future. The Parti Québécois leaders are trying to prove that the economic consequences of Quebec's future independence will be beneficial to French-speaking Quebecers. They think that most French-speaking Quebecers will stand by their nationalist leanings when the benefits of the Quebec nationalist stand become clear.

The debate on independence thus revolves around the discussion of the costs and benefits of Quebec sovereignty. Members of the Parti Québécois tend to consider the costs as minor compared to the benefits which could accrue to French-speaking Quebecers. Quebec sovereignty, in the view of the Parti Québécois, would put an end to the

"If it had not been for the political factor I suppose we would not have been moving out of Montreal." *The Montreal Star*, April 5 , 1977, page H-1. For further comments, see Amy Booth's article, "Business priorities play their part in that flight from Quebec", *The Financial Post*, February 26, 1977, page 32. Also, Don Braid and Sheila Arnopoulos, "Fear drives companies out", *The Montreal Star*, May 4, 1977, pages A-1 and A-10.

costly duplication of public services. In the view of their opponents, it would impose overhead costs which would offset any benefits, and it would put an end to equalization payments. Parti Québécois spokesmen respond that in the long run equalization payments are paid for by Quebec taxpayers. Opponents of the Parti Québécois add that sovereignty would scare away investment. Parti Québécois members reply that the nervousness of small investors is caused by a state of uncertainty, which sovereignty would resolve.

The final argument of the Parti Québécois is that, in a sovereign Quebec, all governmental decisions applying to Quebec would be made by Quebecers. The question then arises of the immediate costs involved in moving part of the federal bureaucracy from Ottawa to various locations in Quebec. How will the federal government's assets and liabilities be divided and what will happen in the Canadian North? According to Parti Québécois leaders, the problem is not that complicated. Quebec's share of federal assets and the federal debt will be approximately 25 per cent. The costs of moving French-speaking Ottawa civil servants who want to come to a location in Quebec will be less than three per cent of one year's budget for the government of an independent Quebec.

Parti Québécois leaders have a reply to every major question. They are seeking Quebec's sovereignty in order to satisfy what they perceive to be the needs of French-speaking Quebecers. In their view, French-speaking Quebecers run no risk of being the losers, because they are not the owners. Owning very little, they have very little to lose—and much to gain.

In a sense, the struggle which is developing in Quebec is primarily one between the new social classes, who really do have much to gain, and the traditional élites, both French and English. On one side, are unionized workers and college graduates. On the other side, are the business community and its professional associates. In another sense, this struggle is between "integrists" and "pluralists". The "integrists" include many Parti Québécois activists, while the "pluralists" are typified by Prime Minister Trudeau. The "integrists" are trying to build a new nation-state, Quebec; the "pluralists" are fighting on two fronts, against Quebec nationalists and against English-speaking Canadian "integrists".

Yet, in my view, a compromise *can* be reached, if only because of the equilibrium between the opposing forces. The Quebec electorate is divided by conflicting concerns: language, social class, age, regional

Economics of Split are Complicated

If the separatists win the referendum we would have to determine how the assets and liabilities of the Canadian federation
would be split up. Those who still cannot face such a possibility
would, I suppose, answer that whatever assets are physically in
Quebec will stay there, and the hell with any further discussions
about the rest!

It is not that simple, as even the most rabid colonialists or
colonized in so many countries have found out over the past 30
years.

Quebec has a share in all federal assets, whether located within
its boundaries or not, because it has paid for it. But it also must
share in the federal public debt because part of it was issued for
the benefit of its citizens. We must, therefore, come to some sort
of an agreement on a percentage to split assets as well as
liabilities.

To simplify somewhat, two percentages are of particular significance. The first has to do with population. Quebec has close to
28% of the present Canadian population. It is an important
figure in the sense that several public services are distributed
roughly according to population. The second significant percentage has to do with personal income, which is the real basis for
so many taxes. Quebec's share comes out to something like 25%.
I respectfully suggest that after a couple months discussions, we
will probably compromise on a highly technical coefficient of
26½%.

Should such a coefficient be confirmed, it will be applied to
both assets and debts.

Quebec Finance Minister Jacques Parizeau speaking to the Ontario
Economic Council.
Source: *The Financial Post*, April 30, 1977, page 21.

loyalty and others. A new balance could develop, and the crisis, now
15 years old, could be settled. However, it is hard to see the solution
in simply re-polishing the British North America Act, because such a
mild compromise would never satisfy the well-organized minority of
those who call for Quebec's independence.

If the clamour of Quebec's pro-independence minority is not quieted, the problems will continue. This pro-independence minority seems willing to compromise, but only as far as "souveraineté-association": its activism can be calmed only through a fundamentally different arrangement between Quebec and the rest of Canada.

Suggested Reading

Arès, Richard. *Nos grandes options politiques et constitutionelles*. Montreal: Les Editions Bellarmin, 1972.

Bergeron, Gérard. *L'indépendance: oui, mais ...* Montreal: Les Editions Quinze, 1977.

Bernard, André. *Québec: élections 1976*. Montreal: Hurtubise HMH, 1976.

Black, Edwin R. *Divided Loyalties: Canadian Concepts of Federalism*. Montreal: McGill-Queen's University Press, 1975.

Brossard, Jacques. *L'accession à la souveraineté et le cas du Québec: conditions et modalités politico-juridiques*. Montreal: Presses de l'Université de Montréal, 1976.

Burns, R. M., ed. *One Country or Two?* Montreal: McGill-Queen's University Press, 1971.

Chodos, Robert and Nick Auf der Maur, ed. *Quebec: A Chronicle 1968–1972*. Toronto: James Lorimer and Co., 1972.

Dion, Léon. *Nationalismes et politique au Québec*. Montreal: Hurtubise HMH, 1975.

Johnson, Daniel. *Egalité ou independance*. Montreal: Les Editions Renaissance, 1965.

Joy, Richard J. *Languages in Conflict*. Toronto: McClelland and Stewart, 1972.

Larocque, André. *Défis au Parti Québécois*. Montreal: Les Editions du Jour, 1971.

Legault, Albert and Alfred O. Hero, ed. *Le nationalisme québécois à la croisée des chemins*. Quebec: Centre québécois des relations internationales, 1975.

Lévesque, René. *An Option for Quebec*. Toronto: McClelland and Stewart, 1968.

Meekison, Peter J. *Canadian Federalism: Myth or Reality?* Toronto: Methuen, 1968.

Milner, S. H. and H. Milner. *The Decolonization of Quebec: An Analysis of Left-Wing Nationalism.* Toronto: McClelland and Stewart, 1973.

Morin, Claude. *Quebec versus Ottawa.* Toronto: University of Toronto Press, 1976.

Murray, Vera. *Le Parti Québécois: de la fondation à la prise du pouvoir.* Montreal: Hurtubise HMH, 1976.

Rioux, Marcel. *Quebec in Question.* Translated by James Boake. Toronto: James Lorimer and Co., 1978.

Simeon, Richard, ed. *Must Canada Fail?* Montreal: McGill-Queen's University Press, 1977.

Thomson, Dale C., ed. *Quebec Society and Politics: Views from the Inside.* Toronto: McClelland and Stewart, 1973.

Trudeau, Pierre E. *Federalism and the French Canadians.* Toronto: Macmillan, 1968.